PARLIAMENTARY
LOBBYING

PARLIAMENTARY LOBBYING

*Putting the business case
to government*

NIGEL ELLIS

Published on behalf of the CAM Foundation

HEINEMANN PROFESSIONAL PUBLISHING

Heinemann Professional Publishing Ltd
Halley Court, Jordan Hill, Oxford OX2 8EJ
OXFORD   LONDON   MELBOURNE   AUCKLAND

First published 1988
© Nigel Ellis 1988

British Library Cataloguing in Publication Data
Ellis, Nigel
   Parliamentary lobbying: putting the
   business case to government.
   1.   Great Britain. Parliament. House of
   Commons. Members lobbying – For businessmen
   I. Title
   328.41'078

ISBN 0 434 90536 4

Printed in Great Britain by
Redwood Burn Ltd, Trowbridge

CONTENTS

Lobbying makes the world go round, and it can help to inform policy makers.

Christopher Huhne, Economics Editor, *The Guardian*, writing in *The Spectator* 5 March 1988.

FOREWORD

Nigel Ellis is one of the leading practitioners of public relations in this country. Until now he was perhaps best known as the joint author of one of the most definitive textbooks on public relations published in this country.

Having updated this recently, he has now turned his attention to the fast-growing area of government affairs. This much needed book sets out to explore the current lobbying scene and offers much sensible guidance for the newcomer as well as the experienced practitioner. He also charts the strong currents and sandbanks that can shipwreck the unwary who venture onto these seas without a compass and maps from the qualified and experienced lobbyist.

As in his earlier book, the author believes in the value of using case histories to illustrate his main points. None of these are more valuable than those that involve the European Parliament, and with 1992 so uppermost in our plans the book is worth reading in this context alone.

The author has a sardonic but kindly view of the processes of government and while his perceptions are often concealed by witty observations these should not obscure their validity or acuity.

I welcome this book on behalf of The Institute of Public Relations and indeed all practitioners of PR. It is a timely publication as the Institute's government affairs group is the fastest growing of our special interest groups. I recommend it to everybody who has an interest in the wider context of parliamentary democracy and our desire for improved communications with government in this country and in Europe.

Tony Spalding
President, The Institute of Public Relations

PREFACE

The impact of legislation on everybody's daily life is constant and all-embracing. The chances are that every citizen and every organization regularly, if unwittingly, breaks the law. Sometimes the law goes back to the Middle Ages; more often it is modern. It often does little harm when the individual transgresses. For the organization, though, whether commercial or not, it can be a serious matter, and too many have discovered the power of the truth that 'ignorance of the law excuses no man, not that all men know the law because 'tis an excuse every man will plead . . .'

Many believe that legislation has become a habit in which we over-indulge. Certainly we are surrounded by Acts, Regulations, Directives and Statutory Instruments whose intentions were probably benevolent but the cumulative effect of which today is often strangulation.

The way we are governed, the forces that shape the collective and individual thinking are all subjects of absorbing interest. Studies of them fill bookshelves. Theories of what-might-be and what-ought-to-be are as plentiful as falling leaves in the autumn.

Democracy, that over-used and little understood word, is at the core of all the debates, since what it means in the end is a society in which all members take part or have the opportunity to take part. Sadly, many people dismiss the discussions, the newspaper articles, the television programmes and the books, on the grounds that they are either not interested or 'have better things to do'. The consequence of this attitude is that they wake up one morning to discover that some newly passed piece of legislation totally alters their lives. Then they are left wondering why they did not know about it and what they could have done about it. This is specially true of men and women in their role as the managers of business enterprises.

This book sets out to tell them how to go about answering the two points. It is a guide to the way Britain is governed. But it is also a book about human behaviour. It is not possible to try to understand how to influence government thinking in all forms without understanding the people who do that thinking. So the book looks at the two main streams of government – the elected and the appointed. It looks at some of the outside pressures that mould and massage the thinking and decisions of both, and then provides the practical advice the newcomer to the scene needs so that he can make his voice heard. To understand the people and the processes is to know how to affect them.

Parliament and the Civil Service are not mere forests of talkers whose denizens do not understand the 'real' world, whatever that may be. I have tried to dispel that illusion.

There is a central message. Maintaining the state of affairs is usually not difficult: changing it is. It needs effort and careful planning, and, above all, time. 'Make use of time: let not advantage slip' is good advice.

Many people have contributed to this book and it is proper that I should thank them.

Some of the case histories in Chapter 7 were written specially. For the others I was given permission to lift and quote from already published material. I, and the authors, hope that readers, especially students, will gain from the experience passed on.

Without Douglas Smith, Managing Director of Political Research and Communication Limited, this book might never have appeared. He gave of his time and skill freely, in particular for Chapters 3 and 11. Peter Hunt, lately Director of Government & Industry Affairs, Coca-Cola Northern Europe, read the manuscript and made valuable comments.

The others to whom I am indebted are: Alan Mattingly, Director of The Ramblers' Association; Warren Newman,

Past-President, The Institute of Public Relations and Director of
PR, National Farmers' Union; Peter Chandler, deputy managing
director, Daniel J. Edelman Limited; Annette Middleton and
Pamela Timms of the SOS Committee and Chilmark Public
Relations Limited; Michael Windridge, at that time Director,
Government Affairs, The McCann Consultancy; Peter Luff,
Managing Director, Good Relations Public Affairs Limited;
John de Mierre, of McAvoy Wreford Bayley Limited; Paul
Taylor, Associate Director, Political Research and Communica-
tion Limited; Evie Soames, Charles Barker Watney & Powell
Limited; The Local Government Information Unit; and Bob
Worcester, Chairman, Market Opinion Research International
Limited (MORI).

Of course I am grateful to them all – but readers should be
more so.

NIGEL ELLIS

1

RESPONSIBILITIES
AND RIGHTS

Government is a fact of life. Modern society has accepted some degree of organization of its affairs as useful, necessary, and perhaps inevitable. In those states where the adult population is given the opportunity to change or re-elect its government at known intervals, voters have the undeniable right and almost certainly the responsibility to attempt to influence the laws and regulations devised by the government or placed on its agenda by the efforts of individuals or pressure groups.

That right and responsibility does not actually disappear even in a state where the government does not stand for re-election. Only the methods are different. Neither is the principle altered in any way because a sizeable proportion of the population normally chooses not to exercise its rights. Failure to do what some might regard as their duty may be reprehensible but is not yet an indictable offence in the United Kingdom.

At the heart of the process of understanding and then trying to influence government lies information. Without information it is impossible for voters to know whether proposed legislation is good, bad, necessary or unnecessary.

Support for greater access to information is growing. A notable adherent to the cause is Sir Douglas Wass, who was permanent secretary to the Treasury from 1974 to 1983. In a lecture at Manchester University, he questioned '. . . whether our normal methods of formulating policy give us, the public and our representatives, the opportunities we are entitled to in a participatory democracy to pass judgement on what is proposed for our good'.

He then offered 'some suggestions as to how the existing mechanisms for opening up policy formulation can be strengthened without imposing impossible or intolerable constraints on the freedom and indeed duty of the government to govern'. Specifically he called for freedom of information (statutory right of access), the creation of a Department of the Official Opposition, greater strength for departmental committees, sharper Parliamentary procedures to allow fuller debate on policy proposals, more specialist consultative committees, a standing Royal Commission which would initiate policy studies and debate, and the devolution of detailed policy-making and implementation to public boards, as existed in the nineteenth century. Coming from someone of his obvious experience and authority, these proposals need careful consideration.

All the information needed, exists, of course. It may take effort and time to acquire it – sometimes it is unpleasantly long and difficult to force government to disgorge information about its plans, but it can always be done in the end. Information on its own, however, may be useless without the knowledge of how to make the most of it.

Therein lies one of the fundamental problems of the modern world. Society becomes more and more complex (more than necessary, many might say). The world becomes smaller and its peoples thus more interdependent. There is more understanding of people's responsibilities to each other. Many forces work to increase stress, ambition, perceived needs and so on, and to create new patterns of behaviour. These and other changes in the way we now live our lives lead to two things: increased pressure on government to introduce new laws and less time for those affected to study them before they reach the statute book.

Consider this. At one time no government needed to devote any attention to the problems of football hooliganism, data privacy or international terrorism. Hooligans were a containable minority. The development of electronic data-processing was at an early stage and the possibility for all sorts of organizations to maintain huge files of personal information did not exist. International terrorism was on a tiny scale.

Indeed the pace of change, if not its actual depth, is now often alarmingly fast. It is even sometimes difficult to remember what apparent social disasters were troubling us a year ago.

Political Decisions

Governments have to respond to these changes. That is the reason for their existence. They are supposed to be there to provide the rest of us with a framework in which we may lead our lives in an orderly, peaceful fashion. They must balance one set of demands against another. Will the general good be best served by incarcerating hooligans in prison or will it be counter-productive? Should higher rates of taxation be used to finance schemes of care for the elderly or is it better to lower taxes and create the conditions in which their families can look after them privately? What is more important: allowing 40-tonne lorries to carry even bigger loads or protecting our disappearing environment against the damage they cause? Where should toxic waste be deposited, and for that matter should we have any truck with nuclear energy generation and all its dangers?

These matters are the stuff of government. They call for political decisions, but they impinge on all of us and are thus important.

Instantly there is the next problem. Running any business organization demands hard work and long hours. The smaller the organization and the more closely identified with it the owner-manager, the greater the time pressure. Yet he is also the person most likely to be both immediately affected by new legislation and most surprised that it has been passed. It is obvious that a change in the law – say an amendment to the Companies Act – affects all companies. But the chairman, managing director, or chief executive of a large company can devote his time to strategy, supported in the knowledge that he has specialized employees or consultants who will study the impact of any change and advise him if there is anything he personally needs to do. The small owner-manager does not have

3

this cushion. For many of them it is a situation in which they can only 'do their best', reacting and responding while simultaneously trying to cope with the host of urgent demands that greet them every morning. For that reason most businessmen decide that it is nothing to do with them and hope fervently that it will all go away. Of course, it does not.

Large commercial companies are by now well accustomed to the need either to bend government action to their will or to mitigate the effects of what they usually regard as totally unnecessary, fanciful, and even crazy legislation. They are often surprisingly ill-equipped to handle the necessary techniques. Small companies look to their trade associations to guard what they perceive to be their interests, but are usually not prepared to spend time studying the guidance papers issued by the associations. Even if they do, a common reaction is to complain bitterly in the golf club at what 'they' are trying to do to 'us'. The complaint rarely takes the form of action.

It is a teasing situation. On the one hand there is the government, elected to an authoritative position and expected to work always for the greater good. On the other there are the voters who have put the government in power and yet clearly give the impression that they wish the government would leave them alone.

There are many explanations, most of them related to the different imperatives of both sides. One distinguished public affairs consultant put it like this:

> ... experience over many years has served only to reinforce my view that there is a generic and occupational antipathy between the marketing and political mind, and for the former to regard government as automatically hostile. The maker and marketer of goods deals in precise performance and measurable results. The politician's role by contrast is open-ended and concerned primarily with states of affairs.

The Hansard Society for Parliamentary Government, in a specially commissioned report 'Politics and Industry – the Great Mismatch', put it in slightly different words but with the same meaning:

4

There is little doubt that many people feel that one of the causes of Britain's problems has been the failure of government and industry to work effectively together. The area where misunderstanding is biggest is that of time scales. On the one hand, politicians introduce industrial policies expecting to see the results at least within their term of office, if not before; on the other, industrialists face investment lead times not determined by the next by-election or general election and perhaps spanning a decade or more.

One of the best summaries of the situation came from Hazel Duffy, a *Financial Times* writer, who said:

The British tend to be woefully ignorant about the way in which their political institutions work. Many businessmen, intent on meeting the day-to-day demands of management, simply do not have the time to work out the intricacies of the Civil Service hierarchy or the committee system at Westminster, let alone the corridors of power in Brussels. They pay their subscription to the Confederation of British Industry, trade associations, chamber of commerce, and hope that these bodies will be their worthy representatives in negotiations with government.

Most of the time that works. But what if there is a more specific matter which arises from the political and administrative processes? For example, a bill going through parliament, or a directive about to be agreed by the Council of Ministers, which will have a direct impact on a particular company. Or, perhaps that the businessman feels he would like to try to influence government thinking in the policy preparation stage? Who should he approach? Which is likely to be the most effective route – civil servant, back bench MP, or the minister?

Some of the largest companies have specialists in government affairs. Their job is to liaise with officials and politicians so that they know what is on the agenda, and help to ensure that their senior people will be given the chance to make their views known. But this is a luxury for the vast mass of companies.

Rights and Responsibilities

True, but somehow unsatisfactory. One government minister made the case for stronger action by businessmen in a speech to a business audience. He said that they 'should dare to be political and become more directly involved in public debate on policy, thereby offsetting the tendency for politicians to be absorbed into the massive state machinery'. He added that businessmen could help politicians by acting directly in the realm of policy and ideas.

The paradoxes remain. Rights and responsibilities are bedfellows. No one really has the right to protest against legislation once passed if he has abdicated the responsibility of making his protest at the time it was conceived or in an early stage. The observer who noted the fundamental difference between the motivations of politicians and businessmen went on to say: 'There is a need for a generic relationship between the politician and the industrialist. (We) need to develop a relationship without a crisis so that (we) do not face a crisis without a relationship'.

In the eyes of many businessmen Parliament is an irritating talking shop, 'the finest club in London', and a natural home for venal, shallow, uninformed seekers after personal power. In a hazy way it is widely felt that since politics is often about trade-offs, the 'one step forward and two back' syndrome, the professionals in it are sinister and certainly not to be trusted. Trading off says: 'If you follow this course of action, it will probably cost you X,000 votes, but if you amend it, you will save at least half of them'. The course of action may be economically or socially necessary, even vital, and the amendment meaningless, but the sound of voting slips with the cross in the right place dropping into ballot boxes is a powerful motivator. Sometimes it is too obvious. As was remarked by another regular observer about the relation between Parliament and business: 'Too many people are ignorant of the workings of Parliament. They act in this ignorance and are often thought to be acting in arrogance'.

The truth of course is that neither side wants to understand the other, because their motives and objectives are not only not the same but can never be the same.

It is probably no accident that few 'captains of industry' have been successful when introduced into government via a safe seat by-election or by appointment to a public service office. They think differently, sufficiently so for it to be extremely difficult for them to make the transition to 'social' thinking. It is probably equally no accident that relatively few members of Parliament have direct business experience. The qualities that produce success in one sphere are not those required by the other.

Since government is with us to stay, it is really to be regretted that the esteem for Parliament has so declined. The rules of the game now seem to be how to find the most effective way of government and business outwitting each other. Unhappily confrontation has yet to prove itself a productive way of conducting our existence.

At one time the two sides seemed to be able to run alongside each other without too much friction. But the world was then a much more innocent place and the pace of life was slower. For the reasons already noted, that has gone beyond recall. Government and business recognize that both must continue and for now appear to feel that the love-hate relationship is about the best they can achieve.

That is not to say that attempts to improve matters have not been made and do not go on being made. Nor does it mean that it is not worth trying. A notable attempt has been the Industry and Parliament Trust (whose work is explained later, p.52). The steady flow of loans of businessmen to the public service, and secondments of civil servants to business, is another. Informal groups of all kinds meet constantly. Trade associations and major industrial undertakings also put in their two-pennyworth.

Yet the suspicion remains. The average businessman, especially once he is 50 miles from London, tends to say: 'I can do nothing about it so I am not going to waste my time trying'.

It is indeed worth trying. More than that it is desperately necessary that the voice of business heard clearly at Westminster should not just be that of the big and the powerful. If it is true (however yet unproved) that the future lies with small businesses, then the society we build must be geared to them just as much as to the national, international and multi-national corporations. The collective voice has much strength but it is not always a correct reflection of views. Aspects of the art of the mob orator creep into the submissions to government by professional bodies and trade associations. Nothing can actually replace the assiduous cultivation of contact between both sides on the broadest possible scale. Persistence is the key. The businessman who writes one letter of protest to his member of Parliament and does not receive a satisfactory answer should not give up. The MP who is snubbed first time by an organization in his constituency must keep on trying to find a way of getting alongside it.

An internal note in one large organization raised the seemingly cynical but actually realistic question: '. . . whether this exercise (developing closer relationship with government) is really worth management's time. What good will it do, and more particularly what good will it do Company X? What will we gain?'

That note went on to say:

. . . in general, the gulf between industry and Parliament is wide and has perceptively widened over the past few years. At the same time Government legislation and involvement in industry has grown. Despite the growing feeling that perhaps there has been too much Government interference, I do not think the situation will drastically change, whatever political party is in power. Nor should we look to public opinion to give us whole-hearted support. In many cases public opinion is ignorant of industry's specific problems and the remedies needed and is always notoriously fickle in its views. For the past few years, too, the public has tended to see the more negative side of industry – pollution, poor quality, bad industrial relations, bad management, high profits, etc. A major exercise in communication is therefore necessary and this cannot be wholly carried out by trade associations, although they have a part to play. It will be up to individual companies to establish themselves. Some major companies have already done this and been rewarded for their efforts.

Does it work? BP, the oil major, maintained that in the mass (morass perhaps?) of legislation affecting their industry in the 1970s the two sides inevitably came much closer together. Although the industry failed to change the direction of the government's policies, it claims that the measures introduced were made workable as a result of the industry's interventions and comments.

Pressure Groups

Whether pressure groups or individual pressure really achieve results is another question. Certainly with some legislation the pressure groups arguing for it had to make unremitting efforts over half a century before they attained their objective. Others can show results over a much shorter period. In the 1960s one bill, badly drafted because hastily introduced to respond to public clamour, contained a clause which, if incorporated into the final Act, would have had a totally unintended effect. It would actually have led to the closing down of a number of companies who were acting perfectly legally, although in an aspect of retailing which some judged to be unwelcome. The drafters of the bill had not sought this effect and it was only the sharp eyes of an employee of one of the companies that brought it to light.

As John Philpot Curran said when elected to office as Lord Mayor of Dublin in 1790: 'The condition upon which God hath given liberty to man is eternal vigilance'. The same can be said of monitoring Parliament and aiming to influence its actions.

Government does not consist only of members of the House of Commons and the House of Lords. These are the elected representatives and the second Chamber. Behind them, sometimes supporting them and sometimes opposing them, is the vast administrative machine known as the Civil Service. In the search for practical and effective techniques for swinging government action in particular directions understanding the role of civil servants is critical. The service embraces hundreds of thousands of public servants who have nothing to do with government policy

9

beyond implementing it. Those who count in this context are a small number at the middle to upper reaches of policy-making departments. They are the ones who have a dual role. They may interpret a government's wishes in the framing of legislation, or they may initiate it themselves. They will give their ministers the material with which to answer Parliamentary questions, to deal with subjects raised directly with ministers by backbench MPs, as well as supplying the background and statistics for government speeches.

Peter Hennessy, one of the most knowledgeable writers on the subject of relations with government, has written: 'Anyone interested in understanding the real, hidden government in Whitehall, as opposed to the visible, semi-artificial version, shaped largely by presentational factors, which dominates life at Westminster – must concentrate on the Cabinet Committees'. If that is true, as it certainly is, it is equally true that it is on information from key civil servants combined with political desires and ability that these committees reach their views.

Another writer said: 'The prime qualification of the modern professional lobbyists, many of them former civil servants or political researchers, is that they know the names of the obscure principals and assistant secretaries who actually write the papers on which ministers decide policy'. Yet a third writer, Sue Cameron of the *Financial Times*, who spent 18 months in Whitehall working in the Civil Service, had definite views: 'Whitehall is an alien land. They do things differently there. Yet they are the ones who award the contracts, decide the grants, recommend the tax changes and frame the new laws that can have a profound effect on your livelihood'.

The whole process is about securing opportunities to put across a point of view to Parliamentarians and senior civil servants so that it is taken into account as they work to order our futures. It is a fundamental right to do this, enshrined in our history. It is more than merely important. It is vital to a healthy and free nation. It needs time and it needs effort as well as familiarity with the methods.

2

ELECTED TO RULE

There is politics and there is party politics. The two are related but should not be confused with each other.

Politics, as defined by the *Oxford English Dictionary*, is: 'The science and art of government; the science dealing with the form, organization and administration of a state or part of one, and with the regulation of its relations with other states'. Party politics, on the other hand, is concerned with convincing voters that one set of policies is better than another, and manoeuvring so that at the time of an election the upholders of those policies are elected. In the process half-truths may emerge on both sides. Indeed they frequently do. Aspirants to a seat in the House will know that some of the policies they advocate are moonshine. Their justification is that if they appeal to the electorate and help a party to win an election, the other, practical, philosophies they espouse will result in a better run state. That may be the reason why politicians are generally held in fairly low esteem, and why the *OED* (again) includes the 1764 definition of a politician as 'a crafty intriguer'.

The fact that much of party politics comprises dubious optimism about the results of the policies advocated, wheeling and dealing, making one concession against the offer of another, and often employing hyperbole or near slander, is not really an argument for its abolition. The business of governing is not to be tied up in neat little packages designed to last for ever and over which there can be no disagreement. Honestly held views about the path to (political) heaven must be allowed free expression. Carlyle's indictment of 'six hundred talking asses' was unfair. In the world of education a teacher turned politician may decide for perfectly understandable reasons and from long experience that comprehensive schools produce the best results and the greatest range of opportunities. Another, for equally valid reasons and with a similar length of experience, may decide that grammar schools must be retained at all costs. They are entitled to advance their views. If they exaggerate in their desire to make a point, who is to say they are wrong or unworthy of public support? Who can say, hand on heart, they have never slightly or even considerably bent the facts to fit the story?

One hesitates to quarrel with the editors of the *OED*, but it is difficult to accept without some discussion that politics, meaning government, is a 'science'. There can be no doubt that it is an art. But if science is taken to indicate precision, then it is not easy to apply the description to politics, party or otherwise. It was R. A. Butler, sometimes labelled the best unelected Prime Minister of Britain, who quoted Bismarck's aphorism: 'Politics is the art of the possible'.

No political party can produce a manifesto which will find universal acclaim or even acceptance. No political party can be composed of people who all agree on everything. As Shaw said: 'They (Mr Everyman and Mrs Everywoman) think of politics as something outside life, though politics are either the science of social life, or nothing'. If that is a sustainable assertion, then politics is too subjective to permit such a handy air of permanence.

We come thus to the point that people deserve their politicians. For a proper understanding of this and its place in the matter of influencing those who are trying to influence us, it may help to reflect further on both sides.

The psychologist Dr J. A. C. Brown in *Techniques of Persuasion* wrote about political propaganda:

One of the weaknesses of the democracies is their failure to understand some of the less rational facets of human nature. It is assumed that most people want political doctrines explained to them rationally, that they cannot stand being bamboozled, that they prefer an easy life to a hard one, and that they inevitably prefer pleasure to pain, love to hate. This may be true under ideal conditions, but in the circumstances of 'quiet frustration' in which most lives are lived it is not true at all.'

The Best Club

There is a fairly general feeling that becoming a member of 'Britain's best club' seduces politicians, wraps them in a cocoon of unreality and divorces them from the real life lived by many of their constituents. It is sometimes assumed that it is only because of the promise of this allegedly soft life that otherwise rational men and women stand for election. Some MPs do sit back and enjoy the undeniably pleasant feeling of comradeship and shared power that is quickly engendered in Parliament. They are then touched with reality, and come to suffer from what has been called the 'arrogance of office'. It is not entirely true. Most MPs start by wishing to serve the general good. The route from which they come is immaterial. The party they join is also immaterial, at least for the purposes of this argument. The story of the two undergraduates who tossed to decide which party each should join since they felt there was not room at the top of one party for both of them is almost certainly apocryphal – even if it was told of two men who both became ministers of state. The fact that most members of the Commons tend to bend the knee to show business, especially during their campaigns for election, merely underlines Dr Brown's comment.

To outsiders the apparent remoteness is noticeable. The late Jack Sewell, at the time a gallery reporter for the *Daily Telegraph*, wrote (*Mirror of Britain*, published in 1941): 'There is sometimes a sensation, as one sits in the Press Gallery, of looking down into an aquarium. At moments one sees Members of Parliament as strange, alien creatures whose activities, however important they seem to be to themselves, have no relevance whatsoever to one's own daily life'. It is still true today.

13

It makes more of an impact on constituents who visit Parliament, either to sit in the public gallery or to petition their member. The Palace of Westminster is an imposing place. It smells of history and power and, to some, privilege. It operates to strictly observed, arcane rules of conduct and procedure.

It is not surprising then that it attracts a certain type of performer, and breeds some special attitudes. It is also not surprising that some who enter the chamber do fall prey to self-aggrandisement and become pompous. Given all that, most generalizations are dangerous allies in an argument. The popular conception of Parliament as a bear garden, cultivated by the media in their search for the excitement that sells papers and improves ratings, does members a disservice. Of course there is a good deal of ribaldry and heckling in the course of question time and debates. Of course there are also many times when the House of Commons is almost empty; and it is true that Friday afternoons are a notoriously soporific affair. But Parliament is actually a fairly hard working place.

Some members go through their Parliamentary career without making a single speech. Some have even gone through it without asking a question from the floor. Some are notable orators – a few are able to fill the House with opponents as much as party colleagues by the promise of an intervention in a debate. Some Parliamentary equivalents of remittance men – banished to the Commons after assiduous service in a local authority or trade union branch because it is the only way of getting rid of them – can be guaranteed to empty the House as soon as they rise. Some attend only seldom, when they feel they can spare time from their other careers. Some spend too much time in the bar. Some are what has been called genuine British eccentrics, devoted obsessively to a single cause for which they beat the drum with monotonous frequency.

Several years ago a former director of public relations in a government department, with long experience of watching the House of Commons at work, remarked: 'There have been dishonest MPs. There are MPs over-susceptible to persuasion, but Parliament has no time for the dishonest or the venal. The

Chambers, and the smoking rooms even more, are great discoverers of character. Those who fail the tacit test carry no influence'.

The 650 Members are, after all, a fair reflection of the characteristics, idiosyncracies, abilities, failings, ambitions and achievements of the rest of the population. They are only human.

Persuasion

Of the poor speakers, Jack Sewell wrote:

> In the dullest, most fumbled of speeches there sometimes lurks an exciting fact, a characteristic turn of thought, a surprising glimpse of a mind which is better than its own technique of expression. And the fact that its owner is too careless, too complacent, or too indifferent to improve that technique matters then not at all.

Of the orators, Macaulay wrote: 'The object of oratory alone is not truth but persuasion.' And that is what Parliament is about – persuasion.

Every political party has certain basic tenets to which it adheres, and which all its active members support. They may object sometimes to particular manifestations of it – for example, Edward Heath's classic 'The unacceptable face of capitalism' – but they will only diverge in relatively small details. As parties develop and circumstances change, new approaches are added. Some of them do truly alter the character of the party sufficiently for it to be noticed by the average voter while he is exercising his divine right to apathy. They may be introduced to try to catch him, but they are more likely to come about because an activist feels strongly about them and wishes them written into the script. Most of them make little difference, but they do feed what the media like to call the right, left or centre wings of a party. Sometimes, though seldom, issues cut across normal party lines to such an extent that a free vote is allowed. They are never issues which will bring a party down from power, but they are usually

15

issues on which perceived public opinion is strong enough to make all parties wish it to be seen that they can bury their differences and 'hear what the people are saying'. A reasonable example is capital punishment, on which it is hardly easy to have a Tory, Labour or SLD 'policy' rigidly observed.

The bulk of the time of the average member goes into unseen work. A survey showed that each member of the House of Commons receives more than 10,000 letters a year. John Heddle, the Conservative MP, wrote: 'Letters are delivered about every subject under the sun, mostly from constituents, but others are circulars from interest groups, bank bulletins, stockbrokers' quarterly statements, company reports, the annual accounts and newsletters from the United Nations Association, and so on. The stream of literature never ceases'.

All members hold regular surgeries in their constituencies, when they listen to and try to attend to voters' complaints, problems, suggestions and demands. Many belong to committees of the House and beaver away at the minutiae of legislation. It is a mistake to believe that because an MP is not regularly featured in the daily papers or in broadcasting he is necessarily not earning his keep. The catchline from the well known wartime radio show ITMA might apply: 'It's not always the ones who make the most noise who do the most work'.

However, this is not an apologia for MPs. The discussion is not about feeling sorry for them or admiring them for their industry and devotion to public service, or even about keeping them informed. It is about influencing and encouraging them to bring pressure to bear on government so that legislation is useful and beneficial and not harmful.

Backbenchers' Role

If one is to believe Woodrow Wyatt, who was somewhat soured by his experiences in the House, the individual member is of almost no account. In his epitaph to his life in Westminster he claimed that 'a short spell in the House of Commons is enough to persuade most MPs that the general run of backbench MP has but a trifling say in momentous affairs. Most suspect in their hearts that the job of an ordinary MP is of no great import to the nation, that it is no burden to accomplish, that it requires no great intellect'.

He further made clear his view that:

... the main and almost only supremely valuable function that MPs alone have is to be electoral delegates to confirm the Prime Minister immediately after an election or to choose a new or alternative Prime Minister . . . These delegates are in turn chosen, not representatively by the nation as a whole but by a tiny handful of self-appointed and self-perpetuating activists in the two great parties in each constituency.

He was writing in 1973, before the arrival on the scene of the Alliance.

It was a harsh judgement and not really supported by much intellectually satisfying evidence. But, as he would instantly recognize himself, he was attempting to persuade and was thus choosing his supporting material with some care.

Grimsby MP Austin Mitchell feels much the same. Reviewing a book by Parliamentary reporter Edward Pearce, he said:

We try, like modern school louts who've taken over a public school, to pretend we are the heirs of Pitt (of Chatham, not Croydon), Gladstone, Disraeli, Lloyd George, and Churchill (I not II). In fact, the chamber is different: theirs was burnt or bombed; politics have moved from Parliamentary to populist. The chamber has two roles, both futile. It is a platform on which the arguments for and against the governments are tested in battle. Yet the battle doesn't reach the people it is meant to educate. This is a closed debating society − until it accepts television and gives itself an audience other than Pearce. The Commons is also the theatre of power, but unlike in the United States the end of the drama is always known because the government controls the Commons through its majority. This role therefore reduces itself to heckling a steamroller.

The fact is that an assiduous MP can have an effect, can achieve change, and make his mark without being a rebel in his own party. He can do it even if he is perennially unlucky in the draw for private bills.

The Speaker has said (*The House Magazine*, 18 March 1988):

I am keeping a list of backbenchers who I have heard swing a debate . . . In the last Parliament I had nineteen of them on my list, and in this Parliament I already have four! . . . the truth of the matter is that no one can actually push things through Parliament unless they win the argument. To those who question that, I simply say 'Remember the Shops Bill'.

At any one time about 100 members of the Commons are either in government or close to it. Someone who wishes to raise something with one of them may then find it difficult. Access to ministers is restricted – by pressure of work rather than by any other reason. A minister, especially if he is in the Cabinet, is unlikely to be able to spend too much time attending to a local issue like the siting of a bypass or the disposal of hazardous waste. That does not mean he will ignore it; if it is large enough, he may pass a query or complaint or document to a ministerial colleague or he may pass it to somebody else in his party qualified to handle it or interested in the subject. In such a situation a backbench MP has a useful role to play in drawing a minister's attention to an issue, either getting a quick answer or having an investigation started. Backbenchers are not to be ignored.

Tabling questions is a well trodden path on the route to information or to discover government attitudes. The frequency with which some members get into this piece of the action is well known. Lists are published from time to time showing that member X has asked an interminable number of questions. The cost of answering questions has been calculated. It is regularly suggested that some members are paid by outside interests to ask a question. It is not ethical, and perhaps to be deplored. At the same time, while one may disapprove of a member's motives, the question itself may be important.

There is nothing to stop members having outside employment. For one thing, it supplements what is still a rather inadequate salary. Much more valuably, it can help a member keep in touch with the rest of the world. Provided he plays by the rules, as most do, by declaring his interests so that any remarks he makes can be evaluated, it is asking too much to expect that an MP should be nothing but a full-time Parliamentarian.

MPs' Backgrounds

The routes that lead MPs into the House are many and varied. The law, education and journalism are the favourites. In the 1987 House there are 87 Members who are barristers or solicitors; 62 from education in one form or another; 49 journalists; 32 from marketing, selling, advertising or public relations; 20 farmers; 16 accountants; 15 miners; but only 5 doctors of medicine. Eighty-five list themselves as advisers or consultants for companies, pressure groups, professional bodies or trade associations. Their educational background is more or less predictable. There are 44 Old Etonians, though only 9 Old Harrovians; 122 went to Oxford, 92 to Cambridge, and 184 to other universities.

It is probably not surprising that they do not have either a great understanding or a great sympathy with business. But, curiously, even when they have been in business before entering the House, they seem often to lose sympathy with it. One specialist, in a report to the large public company that retained him, pointed out:

Four things should be remembered of MPs. Firstly, most of them do not have a detailed knowledge of the technicalities or the workings of industry. At the same time, they have a very wide, if sometimes superficial, knowledge of a number of areas. In discussion therefore one must try to strike a balance between these two points. Secondly, an MP is extremely busy. Thirdly, they are constrained by voting in London. A last-minute flurry of divisions could mean the cancellation of engagements at the eleventh hour. Lastly, they are overloaded with paper. At the same time, briefing can be of immense help if it is relevant, to the point, well laid out, easy to comprehend, and short.

All good advice, to be heeded carefully by anyone trying to gain a hearing. With all the misunderstandings it is important to remember that businessmen and politicians are not always interchangeable, and there is no real reason why they should be.

3

RULING, BUT NOT
ELECTED

Perception of the Civil Service within our framework of government often falls more into the field of parody than fact. Brilliantly amusing programmes such as '*Yes, Minister*' reinforce the long-held British belief that the bureaucrats lead all politicians blindly by the nose. Sometimes this is very true.

There is a school of government affairs advisers who are convinced that worthwhile lobbying work is only conducted in Whitehall. Events at Westminster are purely cosmetic. A case or policy should be argued almost in quasi-legal style before the civil service 'bar'. If it succeeds there, and becomes embodied in a bill, then all will be achieved in the gentle course of time. Parliamentary, even ministerial, interference will be minimal. Victory will have been won in the small back room.

Again there is some truth to this line of thought. The Civil Service is well organized, usually intelligently served, virtually permanent. Ministers invariably have a more fleeting career, and their abilities – dare one suggest it? – can occasionally be less intellectually commanding than one might wish. Even the many clever and hard-working ministerial minds become closely wedded, over time, with their departments. The civil servants are always available in the next room with helpful thoughts or soothing words. Avoidance of blunders, which bring politicians down far more frequently than absence of progress or rational thought, can breed a caution intensely aggravating to the outside world of industry and commerce. But civil servants are past masters at the craft.

21

The relation between Whitehall (representing the appointed) and Westminster (representing the elected) has been well documented. Accounts in books are plentiful, from political memoirs, among which Richard Crossman's diaries are among the best known and thought to be the most revealing, to exposés such as Leslie Chapman's *Your Disobedient Servant* and Clive Ponting's *Whitehall: Tragedy or Farce*. Articles appear regularly in daily and Sunday papers, in general periodicals as well as in more abstruse publications.

They all deal in general with the situation in which politicians are trying to effect change and being obstructed by the over-cautious civil servants. The service is charged with being wasteful, amateur, cumbersome, and self-protective. Senior civil servants, who mostly entered straight from university, are accused of being unable to understand the 'real world' of the wealth creators and its needs. They are regularly pictured as spiders methodically enveloping ministers so that the only decisions taken are those of which the Civil Service approves. As one writer noted:

> New ministers who have never been near a great department of state before need careful tutoring in the ways of Whitehall. But don't those who are truly wet behind the ears sometimes make serious mistakes early on? 'Mistakes?' said one senior official. 'No, they don't make mistakes. They're not *permitted* to make mistakes.'

Businessmen brought into government are frozen out of the magic circle until they slink away disillusioned. When ministers bring in special advisers, they are ignored – ever so politely but still completely. Civil servants are, it is said, the masters of the meaningless euphemism and the non-answer wrapped in stylish language. Examples of Whitehall-speak given in an article in the *Financial Times* included 'Some clarification would be useful', which translates as 'You are talking nonsense', and 'There could be difficulty in timing', which means 'We're going to block you'. None, however, reached the heights of Sir Robert Armstrong's 'economical with the truth'.

22

At the same time the service is praised for its efficiency, professional ability and objective approach. Its capacity for serving the government of the day, whatever its political colour and ambitions, is considered enviable, especially in other countries.

Yes, Minister?

It is all true. But then, many of the same things could be said of large business organizations, especially after a take-over or at the appointment of a new chairman or chief executive. All organizations have a culture and most are resistant to change. When a Civil Service department gets a new minister both must get to know each other. Shortly after the 1987 general election, an article in *The Times* noted:

> As Mrs Thatcher's new government gets down to the task . . . Whitehall's senior civil servants are sizing up their reshuffled political masters. 'We're not interested in what they *think*' one remarked this week. 'That may come later, of course, but there are far more important questions to be asked when new people are appointed'.
>
> The questions, in roughly descending order of importance, are along the following lines. Does the new minister get through the paperwork, not least the boxes filled with Civil Service submissions and reports that he takes home at night? Does he take the advice that officials give him? Does he *listen* to their advice? How good is he at running meetings? What are his relations with the Prime Minister? Does he have influence in Cabinet? And, not least, is he a nice bloke?

The politicians are naturally short-term holders of office; if they have any ability, political rather than managerial, they will either be moved on by their leader, or will want to move on. That is quite apart from the fact that they are limited by having to be re-elected. The civil servants are there for much longer, will be more familiar (perhaps over-familiar) with the problem areas of

23

the department, and will be keenly aware of the need for or advisability of continuity. A minister may well be put into a department whose responsibilities bore him to death, a situation hardly conducive to a harmonious or efficient existence with the officials. If it is going to advance his political career, he will take the post – and then leave as many decisions as possible to the staff. Few ministers have had any experience of the manifold difficulties of running an organization the size of a government department. Anyway, they are under incessant pressure, self-induced as well as imposed, to achieve targets and objectives which may well be far removed from those defined or perceived by the department itself. The tug-of-war is bound to continue, and as is true in so many other contexts truth and salvation are somewhere in the middle.

The minister takes responsibility for his department and must defend it even if he believes it to be wrong. He may then be forced into resignation, but he has no choice but to support his officials publicly, since his own reputation is concerned. In any event, just like the managing director or chief executive of a multi-national company, he cannot possibly know everything; and just as the commercial leader delegates authority to his subordinates, so must a minister. It is thus not surprising, as noted in *The Administrative Process in Britain* (R. G. S. Brown and D. R. Steel – Methuen) that:

> . . . many near-Ministerial decisions are given by senior civil servants who decide whether a concession should be made to a pressure group, whether a piece of legislation should be reviewed in consultation with other departments, or whether a problem should be referred to a committee before recommending any particular way of dealing with it. Ministers . . . expect to be warned about political reaction to a proposed policy. Experience in a particular field sometimes makes civil servants more aware of impending trouble than the Minister himself.

Given that the first steps in the legislative process have been summarized as initiation, definition, consultation and ministerial experience, the key role of the Civil Service is clear. While the party in power may well initiate, who else would define (a need, a problem or an opportunity) and consult impartially? The political decision itself will not have come out of the blue. At least part, if not most, of it will have come from party soundings, supporters' input, and pressure of one sort or another. That will inevitably be biased, however slightly. Judging it fairly has to fall on the neutrals of the Civil Service. It may beg the question of the attitude of a civil servant who votes as an individual for an opposite political philosophy, but there are enough checks and balances normally to ensure an even-handed recommendation. It is unlikely that calls for greater politicization will be heard; the growing tendency to appoint political 'advisers' may well be the nearest the idea will get, even when they are handled as they are currently.

Legislative Initiative

Clive Ponting laid about him in a frenzy, saying that 'Whitehall' comprised a bunch of incompetent amateurs. When someone of his experience and ability, well recognized as a high flyer in the service, makes his criticisms, they deserve close scrutiny. Having received it, many of them are obviously correct. Yet it was interesting that Leslie Chapman, who had himself used his experience to criticize the over-spending of government departments, ended a review of Mr Ponting's book with: ' . . . given the widespread and fundamental weaknesses described so effectively . . . it must follow that a dozen or so pages are hardly likely to be adequate to cover a comprehensive replacement philosophy, structure and method of working for the whole of central government. Ponting would have done better to have developed his ideas properly and devoted a second book wholly to them'. Maybe he will. It is, of course, no excuse to say that a problem is so big that it is hardly worth the effort of trying to solve it, but it does no harm to recognize that it is indeed big.

At the end of it all lie two vital and sometimes overlooked facts. Wherever the intellectual impetus of legislation starts, whether in a political philosopher's mind, in a sudden surge of public feeling, in direct response to a new set of circumstances, with a civil servant or a pressure group, it ends in Westminster. The law of the land as enshrined in legislation is the proper duty of Parliament. Even regulations handed out by a department of state must draw their authority from a law enacted in Parliament.

There will always be attempts to restructure, reorganize, improve and otherwise tinker with the Civil Service machine. Quite right, too. In the meantime the seeker of influence has to work with what is there, just as he will have to work with whatever replaces it.

It is wise not to forget these facts.

The part played by the Civil Service should not be minimized. There are undoubtedly times, maybe many times, when civil servants' acceptance or rejection of a line of thinking about existing or possible future legislation ensures its advance or frustration.

Businessmen's efforts to understand civil servants are a mixture of the formal and informal, the method of the first being, as it were, table d'hôte and the latter carte blanche. There are regular organized meetings, as at Sunningdale and at essentially discreet (a favourite Civil Service word) other locations and in other bodies. Secondment of civil servants to commercial companies is no longer uncommon. The history is also littered with examples of total breakdown in mutual understanding, from the attempt by Edward Heath to turn John Davies from the CBI into a minister to the failure of Victor Paige from the National Freight Consortium to 'manage' the National Health Service successfully. Even Michael Heseltine's well promoted management initiatives came up against a well practised inertia.

Moreover, of course, it is absolutely necessary to understand the nature of the beast. Excellent guidance on how to 'win in Whitehall' was given in a *Financial Times* article by Sue Cameron, who has spent 18 months working in the Civil Service. She wrote:

DO familiarise yourself with Whitehall's hierarchy; have a stab at learning their language; make an effort to sort the official sheep from the departmental goats; maintain contact with bright officials even after they have moved; DON'T be shy of ringing up an official you know; start at the top of the hierarchy (except in the case of a Minister); overlook the regional offices of the DTI; forget that you have something the mandarins want – information; DO give them early warning of problems; remember that having eaten lunch your guest will write down everything you have said and distribute copies, with his impressions of you, to anyone who might conceivably be interested; DON'T be overawed by Ministers; listen to them when they tell you not to make a fuss.

All this advice is well worth listening to.

All this being said, and much accepted, the fact remains that pressures outside Whitehall do make considerable mark. Ministers, even prime ministers, have ignored backbench colleagues at their peril. A majority of MPs will fight furiously for constituency interests if they are convinced of their worth. The 'seat' is after all home base for their own political future. They can win wider sympathy thereby, and accordingly no sensible minister ignores them. Bills have been radically changed, sometimes even suddenly abandoned, because of political pressure stimulated by outside interests, almost overnight.

The media play their part in this. Governments are not immune from hostile, informed comment. No minister smiles at attacks in the heavyweight press or hostile interviews on television and radio. Thus there is another lobbying avenue to pursue.

Timing Approaches

In dealing with the Civil Service it therefore pays not only to consult them early and fully, because their sway is considerable, but it also behoves one to hedge one's bets by winning other allies. Members of Parliament, selected peers, sensible journalists all have their place in the lobbying function. At Whitehall it is quickly appreciated if you have outside support – voices that can speak into the ministerial ear privately; pens that will probe any delays. This is not to advocate bullyboy techniques but simply to suggest how a wise man approaches problems or opportunities with all the support and every ally he can muster.

Every trade, industry, craft or profession enjoys a 'sponsoring' department in Whitehall. That means there is a minister usually below secretary of state level, who is formally concerned with that business – both to support (assuming it is worthy) or report on needs or fears (assuming they are reasonable). More significantly the minister has specific civil servants whose task it is to perform this work for him. These are the key contacts and should be cultivated. In the majority of cases, perforce, they will be found within the Department of Trade and Industry. But if in doubt, ask the DTI for advice.

It is usually fruitless to approach the Treasury on business matters, although many still make the error. Enquiries will invariably be referred to another sponsoring department. Equally, with problems of taxation, enquiries would be directed to a local tax office or VAT man.

Letters to the Prime Minister will even more speedily, though politely, be sent to the sponsoring department concerned. Only the Central Statistical Office, which falls under the Cabinet Office, is likely to be of help with business queries, and it is worth recording that its help can be considerable.

Sensible identification of the department most concerned, and those delegated to the subject within it, are accordingly the very first steps to take. The local MP will be happy to assist here, provided he is not bogged down in detail. In any event, his understanding of specific needs could well be helpful later, should problems then be encountered. Members are always willing to help in opening doors. Understandably they are more reluctant to perform any further work when other duties press upon them – perhaps another reminder that the reality of political and legislative life is at Westminster, as is the source of power. Chasing civil servants to answer constituents' queries is not always the most rewarding way of spending the day.

Trade or professional associations should have contacts both in Whitehall and Westminster as part of their function. If a businessman belongs to the relevant body, then he would be foolish not to explore the help it can offer. The quality and service he will receive from this source differs greatly. Some areas of industry, commerce and the professions have powerful, well organized, well informed associations. Others, sadly, have not. The poor performers can be particularly damaging, since they rarely fail to promise much before falling down on delivery. It therefore pays to make proper discreet inquiries into their standards. The better examples will make splendid allies. They will know the key civil servants, they will have access to facts and figures even more far-ranging than departments with which they deal, and their intelligence network both in the UK and EEC will be extensive.

A difficulty often encountered in dealing with trade associations is, however, their breadth of view. Representing often a very wide range of interests, they can frequently be disbarred from pushing the case of a particular member. Thus, for active lobbying, reliance may need to be placed on one's own efforts. This is not in any way to discount the value of the information and advice available from trade bodies, but the individual must be sure that his special needs and complaints can be best dealt with by them rather than by himself on his own.

Entertaining Civil Servants

Having opened up direct lines of contact with an individual civil servant, how then should you properly proceed? 'Proper' has a distinct and clear meaning and has to do with ethics. Civil servants are public servants and attempts to 'bribe' them are not only wrong but usually a failure. Small 'presents', from lunch to a ballpoint pen with a company logo, are perfectly acceptable, but the wise businessman will make sure he does not overstep the mark. Over-lavish entertainment and favours are not advisable. All departments have their own rules on hospitality, and these can be quickly established. Excessive puritanism is not necessary. An occasional working lunch can be organized, and calendars are not out of order. 'Think before you act' is probably a good rule.

The great majority of business people find Civil Service contacts helpful and constructive. After all, Whitehall is as concerned as anyone to get matters right, even if its pace and urgency occasionally vary. Civil servants recognize those more likely to be in command of facts and figures in their particular sphere. Equally business people should appreciate how the Civil Service needs to be aware of a wider scene and other pressures. It is of course for the businessman to argue his corner, but those understanding other constraints are always welcome.

The principal value of good Civil Service contact lies in the advantage of early consultation. Any government planning legislation will ask interested groups first what they feel – not perhaps on the principle of the proposed action, but certainly on its detail. Once legislation is formed and framed, amendment is more difficult. To influence it at the earliest opportunity therefore makes excellent sense.

Trade and professional associations clearly enjoy such consultation almost as a matter of right. However, their comments may not always embrace the attitudes of their entire membership. Close attention to the detail of any such discussions is wise because action may well need to be taken separately.

Mention of policy brings some final points on Civil Service contact. It is naive to suppose that all policy decisions emerge from the Cabinet or party political think-tanks, however much constitutional theorists state this to be the case. Intelligent civil servants have their say, and can put up ideas through their ministers on necessary activity to be pursued. They are, in short, politically proactive as well as administratively reactive.

If any policy thoughts need to be imparted, there are several courses of action one can follow. For example, a meeting might be sought with the minister's special adviser. They are relatively new creatures (as noted earlier) on the Whitehall scene, drawn from people of the same political affinity as the minister and appointed directly by him. They are not therefore career civil servants but more party political senior assistants and counsellors. As such, they have direct access to, and are in constant contact with, ministers. Policy initiatives or complaints favourably received by them will reach the minister direct, and, if he wishes, the Cabinet also.

Tackling the special adviser, if only to 'sound out' ministerial thinking, is a too frequently neglected lobby path. Much depends on the quality of the person, but the majority are lively and keen to embrace any thoughts likely to be helpful to their master.

A second line of approach in the mysterious middle ground between policy formation and legislative practice lies in a meeting with the minister himself and the staff in his private office. This is far better built around an actual event – the opening of a new plant or office, the presentation of an award – than trying to seek a meeting in Whitehall itself, unless urgency demands the latter course.

To meet the minister quickly, consult the local MP, or, better still, several MPs if sufficient excuse (constituency or otherwise) can be found to mobilize them. No minister can easily refuse to see a delegation led by several MPs with a strong case to put, especially if the MPs come from his own party. The danger lies, however, in an entirely cosmetic encounter: pleasant words, understanding phrases, but no hard action in the end. Winning confidence from a minister and finding an excuse for putting views in a more favourable setting can usually be achieved at a specific event. Ministers are invariably attracted to any occasion which can take them into the field, provided convenient days of the week are proposed (a Friday is preferred) and certainly if good publicity is likely to result.

The Private Office

The sensible course of action here is first to consult with the constituency member concerned to seek his support. It is wise to suggest he should also play a leading part in events. The MP will approach whichever minister is concerned informally. If the reaction is favourable, then a formal letter should be sent to the minister well ahead – 6 months at least – of the proposed event.

Here one needs to understand the function of a minister's private office. At its head is the Principal Private Secretary, usually a civil servant in his thirties selected as someone who could well rise far higher. The private secretary's team includes people, again often potential high flyers, who handle the minister's correspondence, diary and Parliamentary business. They occupy the same office, close to the minister's, and monitor his every action and telephone conversation. They are his minders, but they have sensitive antennae, something the lobbyist needs to realize.

In organizing a function the businessman will therefore become familiar with the minister's team. One of them will draft his speech, briefed by the organizer on local detail, and another will accompany him on the day. It would therefore be wise to invite any civil servant with whom the organizer is already working closely. By the end of the function everybody should know each other much better. The minister might subsequently move posts, and members of his team be promoted. But whatever occurs, a mark will have been made.

The wise host on such occasions ensures he has only one point of real significance to make with his ministerial guest, privately if not in public. That point should be reinforced in later correspondence and pushed home by other techniques, as described elsewhere in this book. It might all well seem a lengthy and time-consuming way of proceeding but there can well be other benefits. The attendance of a minister, and his remarks, if well selected, will certainly spotlight the event in a media sense. Regional television might be attracted when otherwise it would prove difficult. Selected heavyweight journalists could also be invited to join, again with longer-term aims in mind. The effect will then be greater.

Careful selection of targets is as important in Whitehall as in all lobbying work. There are reference books and people to advise one on these. Presentation of the case is also vital. The argument must be simply expressed, backed by hard evidence, and sufficiently sophisticated in approach, i.e. placed in a wider context of government wishes and needs, even if the objective is really to gain a particular priority. The understanding of 'Whitehall' in the broadest sense of the word and what it implies is vital and may be absolutely and totally critical. One may join with authors like Ponting in feeling that the Civil Service needs a complete shake-up but that must never be used as an excuse for trying to bypass it. 'Whitehall' does not operate in any theological or ideological vacuum. Other pressures can be brought to bear on it, and should be cultivated just as shrewdly. The impact will then be far greater.

4

PARLIAMENT AND INDUSTRY

The popular view of the Houses of Parliament, especially the Commons, is very likely summed up in an article published in *The Evening Standard* in 1986. Written by a 13-year-old schoolgirl who spent a day in the House, it said: 'On the initial behaviour of MPs: less of the flapping of books, jeering and open-mouthed slumbers would be beneficial. More order, less cock-a-hooping MPs loving the sound of their own voices wouldn't go amiss'. She went on:

> There was a general crossing and uncrossing of legs, smoothing of shiny heads, and conversation in the background creating a hubbub. Doors flapped as some who had apparently already had enough beat a head-dipped retreat. When an occasional MP had the guts to state his opinion in a way to get noticed, the opposition is quick to respond with jeers and laughter, all against the rather childish background conversation. If I were asked to vote tomorrow I would find it difficult to choose between any of them. Every issue has its good and bad. They should be thinking whether the idea would suit the majority of the population.

While making allowances for both her age and probable degree of naiveté as well as the predilection of popular papers to run 'yah-boo' articles, there are many considerably older and presumably wiser people who would agree with her.

It is not a view confined to this country. As just one illustration of the general low level of regard for our legislators, a journalist in a German paper remarked:

> Ritual dictates that an MP talks big even if he doesn't know what he is talking about. After all, the parliamentarian is expected to satisfy his party's supporters and make political adversaries look uninformed and irresponsible. (There is) a spreading parliamentary mediocrity and a declining force of intellect and even independence of mind. The number of competent experts is declining and the number of political professionals is increasing. These professionals are often called *ausgebufft*, which could be roughly translated as 'shrewd customers', a quality some even regard as political virtue.

Much of the same can be found elsewhere, from the late Peter Sellers' political speeches composed of meaningless generalities to Barry Humphries' Australian Culture Minister Les Patterson.

If the experiment of televising the Commons turns into a permanent feature (not at all unlikely) the nature of the House and its debates will, without doubt, alter. Whether for the better is open to doubt.

When Enoch Powell failed to get re-elected in 1987, he was asked to look back over 37 years in the House. He said:

> I believe that a higher proportion of members in 1950 were independent . . . in the sense that they could not be bribed or brow-beaten by government or leaders. Those were the days when that fabulous species, the knights of the shire, actually inhabited the parliamentary forest . . . (and) another fabulous species, 'the horny handed sons of toil'.

Noting that 'the money factor' was different then, Mr Powell went on:

> In all generations it is alleged that the good manners and behaviour of the House of Commons have deteriorated. I

cannot bring myself to agree. Indeed, if there has been any change, I would guess that though dress is decidedly more informal, even to the point of intentional sloppiness, behaviour in general is less rather than more unkind than it used to be . . . This has brought me at the end to something which has not changed and which with starry-eyed faith I believe never will – the incredible, almost supernatural power of debate in the place. Like the psalmist I have been young and am now old; yet have I not seen the Commons take a subject and debate it, even in the often mistakenly derided 'thin house', without all concerned, government and critics, experts and tyros, having learnt and understood something by the end which they did not at the beginning. I cannot explain why, but it always happens. Without it our public life would be a poor thing.

As I have noted elsewhere, MPs can and do work extremely hard, though much of it is unseen. However, they should all be paying attention to the electors' attitudes and considering how they can raise their standing. The community in its various groups wishes to influence Parliament, but then Parliament wishes to exert influence over the community. For business, the matter of influence is not a 5-minute or 9-day task. It is a long slow grind, demanding absolute attention to detail, the fullest possible understanding of nuances and shifts of opinion, and a fine sense of timing. That is probably one reason why many businesses decide not to bother.

Meeting Members

Because meetings between those who seek to influence Parliament, government and backbench MPs are so often a dialogue of the deaf, both sides need to work harder to turn up their hearing aids. Both can be guilty of entrenched attitudes, and society would certainly benefit if they recognized that fact more quickly. Progress in these areas depends on learning each other's language, which is not as difficult as it might appear at first sight.

On the Parliamentary side the ability of MPs to be high on rhetoric and low on specific commitments, especially at election time, is well known. As one commentator wrote, 'One of the most widely practised arts of politics is the ability to show interest on all occasions and to act on only a few'. Hedging of one's bets is a favourite political game, as it is for political tipsters. It is pleasing to be able to claim credit for having prophesied that something would happen, or actually to have made it happen, by quoting from earlier speeches or articles, possibly out of context. There may be no real harm in this, once it can be spotted and recognized for what it is. Politicians are well versed in speaking, something at which many businessmen fail. They are also adept at being quick mentally, learnt from dealing with hecklers at meetings as well as interrupters in Parliament.

Learning the words and their meanings is critical. Mrs Thatcher was unusually revealing when she was interviewed by the *Financial Times* and said: 'We came across – sometimes you get it in politics – a political feeling which you just cannot at that time overcome and then you have to say "All right, we will just have to put it on one side at the moment".' (The curious grammar probably means the remark was transcribed straight off a tape recording, but the sense is clear.)

The businessman has to remember that politics is about power. The programmes advanced by a party are fundamentally important, since they indicate, even if in double or even treble speak, what the party stands for so that the voter (including businessmen thinking of what will benefit their companies as much as what will benefit them individually) can decide who will get his tick. However important the programmes are, however, they have to be sold to the electorate, just as much as the later adaptations introduced in the light of expediency or experience. It might indeed seem to suit politicians to have a half-informed set of voters who are also apathetic, but fortunately this does not seem to be the trend. Experience shows that more people than before are now aware of the problems facing society and needing corrective political action. Nowadays very few people at any level of society or class, or of any persuasion, could not put their finger on the major problems of the day and even agree what they are. No matter that their solutions may be totally impractical or simplistic. It may be a coincidence that MPs have not all responded to this growing awareness and have preferred to remain often in the cocoon of their generalized and sometimes quasi-legal use of words and phrases.

As Humpty-Dumpty said to Alice, 'When *I* use a word, it means just what I choose it to mean', so the politician might say, 'When I say I will solve unemployment, I don't actually mean I will solve it. I only mean I will go on saying I will solve it, in the hope that something will happen to solve it so that I can then claim the credit'. It is worth repeating what was said earlier: there are political solutions and business solutions and they do not often go together.

Research Results

On the other side is the politician trying to understand what the businessman is telling him. The 1986 MORI (Market & Opinion Research International) opinion survey of MPs contained some interesting material. It set out to investigate the attitudes of MPs towards business and industry generally, a range of particular industries and companies, the criteria on which organizations are assessed, individual organizations' relations with Parliament, factors which promote good relations between organizations and Parliament, and sources of information used by MPs.

In evaluating the factors affecting the judgement about companies one Opposition Member summed up the general attitude: 'Profitability and good industrial relations. Not in one order or the other. They must go hand in hand as equals and everything else stems from them.'

Just over half of the respondents (54 per cent) cited industrial relations as the key to judging a company; nearly the same proportion (51 per cent) went for profitability and financial performance. Among all respondents a quarter mentioned the need for a company to be actively aware of its social responsibility. As one Conservative put it:

Are they conscious of the necessity to communicate with the public and do they take seriously the objections of the public on issues like conservation of the environment and so on? Do they work conscientiously with the local people to promote the welfare of the neighbourhood? Do they take an interest in what's happening in their neighbourhood and do they encourage people to take an interest in them? If the answer to all those questions is yes then I will approve of them. If the answer to any of the questions is no then I may find myself trying to approve.

A shadow minister from the Labour Party had a slightly different view:

Worker relationships should be through properly organised trade unions. Many companies are highly successful, some are still in the 19th century. It's evident when I go around and firms say they've been through a difficult period, but they've taken the workforce into full consultation, had to have redundancies and re-organize, are now getting back on the road and are astounded by the co-operation of their own workforce which is something they've never even attempted before and the trade unions on their side have come into a difficult aspect for the first time and are actually helping to make decisions. That's why I am fully in favour of planning agreements between managements and workers.

One can easily forgive the degree of party position-taking in the responses. In the end they were not that far apart.

There were many minor issues which produced fairly standard replies or comments. Table 1 shows them.

Some of the comments are also worth recording. Some referred to the environment. 'Whether they are polluting the local environment' (Conservative), and 'Attitude to environment by the site they occupy and the state it's in, whether they provide a product which is environmentally safe, whether they package in a friendly way to the environment, throw away, pollution, that sort of thing' (Opposition MP).

39

Table 1 *What are the most important factors you take into account when making your judgements about companies?*

	All (112) %	Conservative (69) %	Opposition (43) %
Industrial relations/strike-free record/involvement of workforce	54	42	(74)
Financial track record/profitability	51	(58)	40
Quality of management	36	39	30
Social responsibility/awareness	25	19	35
Public image/reputation	22	22	23
Quality of product/service	21	23	19
Market share/growth record	21	19	23
Efficiency	17	16	19
Their overseas market/energetic performance in export markets	16	13	21
Competitiveness	15	16	14
Personal knowledge/experience	14	13	16
High morale/sense of pride within company	13	10	16
Employment potential	13	10	16
Quality of marketing	10	9	12
Enterprising/developing its own ideas/innovative	9	10	7
Amount devoted to research and development	9	10	7
Long term planning	8	9	7
Flexibility/ability to diversify	7	7	7
Contribution/commitment to the UK	7	4	12
Level of new investment in the company	6	4	9
Quality of communication	5	7	2
General success	5	6	5
High productivity levels	5	6	5
Forward looking training policy	5	4	7
Technological competence	5	3	9
Industrial sector they are in	3	1	5
Contribution to political party	2	1	2

Source: MORI

40

References to a company's financial track record, including 'balance sheets' and 'dividends', were made by one in two MPs. Conservative MPs, not surprisingly, tend to be more likely to judge a company this way than do Opposition MPs. One in five members refer specifically to a company's market share and growth record, e.g. 'Whether the directors have any shares themselves. Whether their shares are likely to go up rather than down' (Conservative MP), and 'Well, the first thing I obviously go for is the size of their profits and indeed their general success or failure' (Conservative MP). Similar comments include: 'Their first job is to make a profit, pay dividends and pay their workforce' (Conservative MP), and 'Well, the first thing I look at with the companies is the balance sheet. I don't think one can make any judgement about any company till one's seen the balance sheet' (Shadow minister).

Linked with profitability is efficiency. One in six MPs would judge a company by its efficiency:

First thing to look for is efficiency in the company that's reflected in the annual report. One of the important things for me is to visit a company and talk to the workforce to assess industrial relations; then if they're producing efficiently with a happy workforce, that's a hallmark of success in my book' (Opposition MP).

Attitudes Formed

More than one in three MPs judged a company on the quality of the management. Here are two opinions: 'The quality of the management, their ability to plan, know where they're going and be able to demonstrate it' (Conservative), and 'When I think about British companies the most important thing in the front of my mind is how modern and up to date the management is and how they are trying to reduce costs' (Opposition MP).

The quality of a product or service provided is likely to be under scrutiny by one in five MPs. The general attitude expressed is that the consumer should 'come first'. Comments included: 'And there is of course the integrity of the product. Not conning the market' (Opposition MP), and 'Reliability and competitiveness of its products in the areas where it operates. I judge as a consumer' (Conservative MP).

The importance of a company recognizing its functions as an employment provider was pointed out. However, the balance between providing jobs and being competitive was noted. In view of the generally held feeling that reducing unemployment is possibly the most intractable but also the most important task facing any government at this end of the twentieth century, it is slightly surprising that the employment potential of a company was placed fairly low down in the list of factors taken into account when forming a judgement.

The survey continued with an enquiry into the ways of forming a good relationship between business and Parliament. One in two MPs referred specifically to establishing personal links between organizations and Members. An effective way of doing this is to identify Members who have an interest in the company and to approach them and/or the constituency MP. Once relevant contacts in the House had been established, communications should be maintained frequently but written material kept to a minimum:

> So build up a relationship and keep in touch with that Member. Wherever a company is operating, they have got a Member of Parliament and the first thing is that once, say, a Member has been elected very quickly they will contact that Member and start to build up a relationship (Opposition MP).

> They have to target MPs in order to identify those likely to have a special concern/interest in that industry or business type. Don't send general stuff to everyone, but specialised stuff to those who need to know. And I think they should send shorter, more specific stuff. Long general stuff is of no interest except to people passionately into that particular area (Shadow minister).

Working through the constituency MP. Unless it is of particular interest, there is not much point in asking MPs to lunch or sending letters. Always get in touch with your local Member, or identify those MPs with interest in your field . . . on a local basis, not centrally as it is frowned on (Conservative MP).

They should study individual Members and their concerns and make a personalised approach, instead of wasting resources on generalised handouts (Conservative MP).

I suppose contact is what matters. MPs like being briefed. It's an enormous help if someone approaches you and alerts you to problems. I have, for example, a big defence contract which was in my part of xxxxx and it's just enormously important to have direct contact with those companies to discuss, to know what is coming up, know what their fears and expectations are . . . By and large it is easy to spot MPs who have an interest, either a proven interest in an area or a constituency connection with a particular industry and I think the important thing is to cultivate that interest (Shadow minister).

Ironically, they should cut down on the amount of unsolicited mail, or, if they send it, make it much more concise. I think certainly that, with MPs who have either a constituency interest or a subject interest a regular (though not necessarily very frequent) personal contact is the best; visits or meetings, face to face, in either direction, visits to the workplace or them visiting us here (Opposition MP).

Circulars are disliked and go into the waste paper basket (Shadow minister).

Brief them briefly and often. Draw MPs' attention to constituency ties (Conservative MP).

Those that keep me informed of what it is they are trying to do to serve the needs of the people I represent I value most (Opposition MP).

43

If it's a constituency interest then I identify that with my own job as a Member of Parliament. I do my best to help promote their goods (Conservative MP).

Optimum Contact

It is important, the survey continued, for a company or business organization to establish an optimum degree of contact, for infrequent contact is as negative as too frequent contact. One in three MPs advised regular contact and not only when problems occurred. However, others preferred companies only to write when something important happened. Essentially an MP wants to know facts and not simply after something has happened:

Now very often at the local level companies don't come to me soon enough. A problem is looming by the time they make contact and by then it may be insoluble. It's just possible that if I'd been involved earlier and got the relevant Minister involved I might have been able to help. I welcome their contact. Big national companies are often good at it. They keep in close touch through all party groups (Opposition MP).

If there is a particular crisis coming up, it's all a matter of just keeping people informed and in touch. I like knowing something about a particular industry. It's important to me, and the best way of doing that is coming in and talking to me (Shadow minister).

Table 2 provides more detail.

When asked about their sources of information MPs had this to reveal. Personal visits to company factories or premises (mentioned by 72 per cent of respondents) and articles in the press (70 per cent) were found to be the two most useful sources of information on companies and business organizations. More than two MPs in five mentioned their own constituents as a useful source of information and the same proportion referred to friends and acquaintances in business. Direct contact with the company was mentioned by at least one in three MPs: 36 per cent found company management (other than PR departments)

Table 2 *What are the most important things companies and business organisations can do to develop and maintain a good relationship with Members of Parliament?*

	All (112) %	Conservative (69) %	Opposition (43) %
Establish personal links	50	(55)	42
Brief MPs with constituency interest	40	41	40
Regular contact	33	28	(42)
Invite MPs to visit	31	(36)	23
Only write when important	24	23	26
Identify which MP is likely to be interested	23	25	21
Keep MP informed	22	22	23
Write precise/short letters	21	17	26
Arrange (informal) meetings	16	14	19
Make us aware of problems	13	12	16
Come to Westminster	12	9	16
Do not only contact when there are problems	11	9	14
Communicate/liaise	10	12	7
Provide accurate information	10	9	12
Communicate through CBI/representative organisations	9	10	7
Spend less money on wining and dining	8	6	12
Send good literature	7	4	12
Lobby MPs better	6	6	7
Issues should be current	6	0	16
Involve MPs in company	4	6	0
Do not approach everyone	3	1	5
Provide transport to and from meetings	2	3	0
Other	12	12	12

Source: MORI

useful, while 29 per cent found company PR departments and press releases to be a useful source of information on companies and business organizations. For 1986 in relation to 1985, the importance of pressure groups had risen by 11 points to 24 per cent. Meanwhile only half as many MPs mentioned the CBI (16 per cent in 1986) or fellow MPs (13 per cent) as useful providers of information. However, when looking at trends, one should note, said MORI, that the list shown to MPs in the 1986 survey contained only 22 sources whereas in 1985 there were 36, in 1984 37 and in 1983, 33. While this was thought unlikely to affect the order of sources found to be useful, it could affect the number of sources mentioned by any particular member.

As for views from both sides of the House, Conservatives were significantly more likely to mention friends and acquaintances in business (54 per cent) than were Opposition members (28 per cent). This has been a continuing pattern emerging from surveys of MPs since 1984, said MORI. Conservatives were also more likely than the Opposition to find the CBI a useful source of information. In the past few years, however, the CBI was not mentioned significantly more by any particular party. The third source of information mentioned more often by Conservatives than by the Opposition was government ministers. This difference did not exist in surveys over the previous few years. Opposition members were more likely to find the TUC or trade unions useful than were the Conservatives. This has been a continuing trend in the MORI surveys since 1983.

Useful Sources

After stating which sources of information they found most useful, MPs were asked which sources they had used in the previous month for information about companies and business organizations. This question had not been asked of MPs before 1986.

The two sources used by at least one in two MPs were articles in the press and personal visits to the company's factories or premises. More than one MP in four had found information during the previous month from the following: friends and acquaintances in business, company management (excluding PR), PR departments or agencies, constituents, annual reports and radio and TV. Significant differences between the Conservative

46

and Opposition reflected those in the previous question. Conservatives were those more likely also to have acquired information from government ministers, from the CBI, from Civil Service departments, and from the Industry and Parliament Trust. Opposition Members were more likely than Tory MPs to have received information on companies and business organizations from the TUC or trade unions.

To assess the survey, it is necessary to give a profile of the sample. See Table 3.

Apart from studying the sample it is also necessary to remember that MPs seldom say anything in public without an eye on the Whip's office, the constituency newspaper(s), and other possible sources of criticism or praise. Yet for all that the survey appears to show that MPs do have an appreciable degree of interest in industry, an awareness of some of its problems and an ability to match political and commercial solutions.

This finding is frankly suspect. At one private meeting the day after two of the most successful and highly regarded 'captains of industry' had criticized the Conservative government for its economic policies four senior Conservative MPs on the fringe of government office dismissed the businessmen's comments with 'Of course, they don't know what they're talking about'. Up to a point this reflects the simple fact that members of the party in power must defend it, especially if they hope for preferment. Only when they have fallen off the promotion ladder, or been pushed off, can they take a totally independent view and appear to judge each case on its merits.

Opposition creates different attitudes. Members of a party seeking power are more likely to be sympathetic to a business case, on the grounds that a willing ear may produce votes.

There is of course the view that backbench MPs are merely vote fodder for their leaders, whether in power or hoping to be. There has to be some truth in this, but it is not a universal truth. In every Parliament there are a few members who stand out because of their clear and entire honesty and dedication to a principle (or what they see as one). They are the members who devote their Parliamentary career to one subject rather than

Table 3 *Sample profile*

	Number 112	% 100
Conservative		
Total	69	62
Minister	6	5
Backbench	63	56
Opposition		
Total	43	38
Labour	39	35
Shadow minister/Opposition spokesman	16	14
Liberal/SDP Alliance backbench	4	4
Backbench	27	24
New Members	3	3
Trade Union		
Member	47	42
Sponsored by union	24	21
Company sponsored	3	3
Experience		
In industry	56	50
In commerce	69	62
Neither	25	22
Region		
Scotland	12	11
North	36	32
Midlands	25	22
South	39	35

Source: MORI

seeking improvements across the board, looking for opportunities to raise discussion in their chosen field, and always acting on their own. Some may have sought election because they saw the House as the best platform from which to act. Others may have come to it after election. Some are, frankly, bores. But more impress the House with their integrity and are able to gain all-party support. Some are a constant problem for government, with their nagging, but if they persist, they demonstrate the truth that one man if so moved can change the world. It would be invidious to pick out particular MPs but perhaps one outstanding example worthy of mention is Jack Ashley, the Labour Member for Stoke-on-Trent South.

Watching Performance

Watching Parliamentary performance to identify MPs of this kind is essential to anybody seeking influence.

The ability of individual members to shift opinion in this context depends on acceptance that they are obviously acting for what they believe to be the common good, ignoring party divisions and personal advancement. It should not be confused with the MP who suddenly appears constantly in the press (articles or letters to the editor) or on television or radio programmes. He may in the former instance be trying to bring himself to the notice of the party leadership at whatever moment he reckons will start him moving upwards, or in the latter he may just be a good entertainer. As like as not he will have decided that he is never going to get into the magic circle, and may not even retain his seat at the next election. In those circumstances he is wisely carving out a second career and source of income. Whatever their motives, MPs in this category seldom have any influence and are best left alone.

It is possible for one member acting on his own to seriously embarrass a government and even bring it to the point of downfall. Unlikely, but possible. Again from the 1983 House one has to remember Tam Dalyell leaping out of his Scottish castle regularly to accuse the government of misdeeds. Although he failed to force the government to actual defeat, he certainly had an effect on its conduct.

Oppositions are always looking for chinks in the government's armour so that they can draw blood with pinpricks. Governments thus have to have ready well honed emergency plans for dealing with the unexpected. In Mrs Thatcher's second term of office she was unusually prey to the unexpected – from the 'sinking of the Belgrano' to the Westland schemozzle, and taking in the resignation of Cecil Parkinson on the way.

These are moments that any effective pressure group should look out for. When a government is under heavy attack, it looks for quick ways to restore its popularity. That may provide an opportunity to drive home a point, to attract attention, or, with luck, to achieve a commitment.

It should not be pretended that results come from opportunistic action, for legislation is neither conceived nor achieved overnight. But there are times in the life of any administration, whatever its majority, when it is vulnerable to pressure. They are not frequent, but it is as well to be conscious of them when they do happen and to try to extract the maximum possible advantage from them.

Perhaps surprisingly, parties are less susceptible in the period before an election than just after they come to power. There is a touching belief that election manifestos are a binding statement of intentions instead of a basis for negotiation. A government preparing to go to the country has made up its mind on the broad issues on which it will fight. The opposition will have done the same. Trying to tie either down to specifics, even on really big issues, is usually fruitless. Better to wait for the result of the election to see how both sides amend their policies before deciding where and when to start trying to exert pressure.

That deals with 'politicians-speak'. At the other end of this particular hot-line is 'business-speak'. It is just as important for the politicians to try to decipher it as for the businessman to break the political codes. All understanding depends on both sides making an effort. Business language has just as much jargon as in any other section of the population. A quick study of the speeches from the floor at a CBI conference shows a depressing familiarity with stock phrases from management textbooks – what Ernest Bevin, Foreign Secretary in the immediate post-war government, would have dismissed again as 'one damned clitch after another'. Businessmen who accuse politicians of verbiage are throwing stones in a glasshouse. When a businessman asks for government help, he is almost invariably acting on a narrow front of self-interest. This remains true even when a view is presented by a professional body or trade association. The politician has to learn to recognize this by making himself at home with business language. The goose and the gander need to be his pilots.

For all that, neither language is all that difficult to follow. The chances of both sides speaking the same language, or using words with a mutually accepted meaning, may be remote, but there is no such thing as a verbal chasm that cannot be bridged. Not, at least, in this context. It is all a matter of making the effort to start from the same point, which can sometimes call for a mutual leap forward and sometimes two or three steps back.

There is a different debate to be held on relative importance – should nationally crucial decisions be prompted by political considerations or those of business? The quick answer is that 'circumstances alter cases', but that is too facile. At the end of the eighties Britain stands in an awkward position. Political decisions seem to be creating a framework in which manufacturing industry is being killed off while industry itself seems to do little to protect itself. Politicians blame manufacturers for being uncompetitive and urge them to learn cost control. On the other hand manufacturers see government awarding nationally vital contracts to foreign competitors and allowing imports to flow in at increasing rates. Neither side appears able to fathom the other's motives or imperatives.

It is because our national future is at stake that it is so desperately necessary for the dialogue to take place regularly, purposefully, and with mutual benefit. There are many people in Parliament of small intelligence but great ability. Neither fact automatically disqualifies them from serving their country well, but they do need balanced information – and industry leaders must see that they get it.

Lastly it is important to pay a tribute to those who had the vision and foresight to form the Industry and Parliament Trust in 1976. They found that only about 15 per cent of MPs had any direct industrial or commercial experience, a figure which has hardly changed since. It should also be remembered that the experience itself may well have been on the bottom rung of the ladder, and possibly not very useful or material to the level of understanding an MP ought to possess. Accordingly they set up a fellowship scheme, financed by participating companies, under which members of the Commons and Lords, clerks to the committees of both houses, and MEPs spend 25 days, spread over a period of normally up to 18 months, attached to companies. They see all the company's operations and sit in board and planning meetings. The whole process is conducted on the basis of confidentiality. The system has mutual value. Fellows learn a bit about industry while industry learns a bit about Parliament. Possibly the most striking evidence that the idea was worthwhile is the fact that similar schemes have been set up in ten countries in Europe and the Commonwealth.

5

DOES PRESSURE WORK?

Does pressure work?

The simple answer is that if it did not, there would not be any pressure groups. Because it can and does, groups with a mind to change or maintain some existing order proliferate. The growth in their number in the last 20 years or so might suggest that people not only believe they have a chance of influencing government but that they actually want to try. Apathy is not universal. Pressure groups, defined as 'institutions trying to influence policy without accepting the responsibility of government', have multiplied as a direct result of the ever-increasing intervention of governments in the economy.

It is arguable that any group of people brought together because they have like interests can be called a pressure group, whether they want to change something or preserve it. The Directory of British Associations lists more than 1,500. In a political context, more than 500 are currently in existence in Britain, excluding trade unions. W. N. Coxall published a chart of what he labelled as the leading sectional and promotional groups in Britain – the former 'based on occupation' and the latter 'arising out of a shared cause or attitude'. Most of the 54 sectional and 66 promotional groups he included are familiar to ordinary people and are regular occupants of space in the media. Some groups are explicitly formed to sponsor, introduce, alter or get rid of legislation. Transport 2000 is one example, as are the Howard League for Penal Reform and the Abortion Law Reform

Association, of which more later. Some are formed for idealistic or emotional reasons – EXIT, Friends of the Earth, Lords Day Observance Society, or the League Against Cruel Sports. Some plod along for years without achieving much public attention, and are then suddenly drawn into the limelight, like the Anti-Apartheid Movement, formed in 1959 and hustled into prominence in 1986. Some continue to be listed long after they have any realistic chance of achieving their objectives. The Anti Common Market League, born in 1961, must now feel it is promoting a fairly hopeless cause. Yet others achieve their task and then alter their *raison d'être* – the Socialist Health Association, for example, was formed in 1930 to work for the establishment of the National Health Service and now exists to 'work for the improvement of the Service and prevention of ill-health'. There are also pressure groups within all political parties, pulling and pushing the leadership in the direction they want.

A final category is composed of those bodies who devote a good deal of their time and effort to presenting their members' and supporters' case to Parliament. They sponsor MPs, they meet as many as possible, they submit written proposals, and they make no secret of their intention to have a structure that gives them what they want. The British Medical Association, the National Farmers' Union, the British Road Federation, the Law Society, the Confederation of British Industry and the Institute of Directors are all outstanding examples of organizations adept at and highly experienced in keeping government aware of their demands.

It may be no accident that these, and others, are largely successful. They command large sums of money (which is only partly relevant) and have full-time professional staffs (which is). They are also dealing in matters that lie at the heart of British life – health, agriculture, distribution, the law and manufacturing. What they do and hope to do affects every citizen (equals voter) every day. What they want is thus a matter of deep concern to government, opposition, and back-bench members. However, that is not the end of the story.

In the 1983 House of Commons, not at all an unusual one, 93 members were solicitors or barristers, 54 were teachers, 62 were journalists or from advertising or public relations, and 20 were farmers. This last figure conceals those in farming constituencies, a vital fact to remember in trying to assess the strength of sectional interests. The figures should also take into account the declared interests of members – in other words those subjects on which they claim to be expert or in which they maintain a close interest. Fifty-five listed agriculture, 68 education, 22 the law, and 17 media policies. It follows that when anything on these subjects is put to them, whether by a pressure group or from government, there is an instant affinity, not to say sympathy (at times antipathy, of course!).

Ramblers vs Farmers

That is not to suggest that there is anything improper in the approach or the reaction. The point is merely made to show that some pressure groups are almost always bound to succeed, if only because they either represent large groups of electors or because they do not have to spend too much time explaining the details of their case. Pressure groups can also be used by the opposition to embarrass or irritate the government.

At times there is an interesting tug of war. The Ramblers' Association has a long and distinguished history of ensuring that the countryside is open. In arguing for footpaths in the country-side and similar amenities they have clashed with farmers. The MP called upon to take a position on such a conflict may find himself in a dilemma. It is passingly interesting that 76 Members of the 1983 House put down 'walking', 'hiking', 'fell walking' and the like as favoured recreations. It may stem from the need to stamp round their constituencies of course!

Even before the rise of conservationists, protection of 'England's green and pleasant land' was a good emotive issue for an MP to be seen supporting. But ramblers are a diffuse group. Where they ramble is not usually where they vote. Their opponents, the farmers, are very much where they vote. Upsetting them is not to be done lightly. The fact that the Ramblers' Association has had so much success is a tribute to its officers and officials.

Some background on the adversaries is revealing. The Ramblers' Association has only a small head office staff in somewhat overcrowded South London premises, though within walking distance of Parliament (a not irrelevant point), and less than £350,000 (1985) to work with. The National Farmers' Union, on the other hand, has the imposing Agriculture House at Hyde Park Corner, also within walking distance of the House, and £20 million to call on. The Ramblers' Association has four full-time staff in its policy section, one of whose several tasks is to monitor Parliament – the NFU public relations department alone is bigger than that. However, the old boxing adage that a good big one will always defeat a good little one does not always apply.

Alan Mattingly, director of the Ramblers' Association, points out that his organization's strong card is the widespread interest in walking. As at September 1986 there were 5,000 individual members and 610 affiliated local clubs. But it is estimated that 10 million people walk in the countryside regularly. That is a potentially powerful number of voices to be raised 'to protect the countryside'. Voices alone of course are not enough; they have to be marshalled. It was a point noted by Lord Melchett, a member of the Association's national executive committee in his contribution to 'Making Tracks', the booklet that marked the fiftieth anniversary of the Association in 1985. He said:

> The RA's effectiveness depends, in part, on the way we're seen by others, those we have to work with and those we have to influence. I think people involved in the process of government – Ministers, opposition spokesmen, MPs and civil servants – hold the RA in pretty high regard. This is simply because the RA staff know more about footpaths and the law, the history of legislation, the arguments and counter-arguments than anybody else does . . . In the coming struggle I think the conservation side is in relatively good shape. If we take the opposition first, the NFU and the Ministry of Agriculture, Fisheries and Food are the major force opposing conservation in general, and the RA in particular . . . it is difficult to distinguish between the NFU and the Ministry in this context.

They always claim to be at loggerheads but generally this is a question of being at loggerheads over whether to spend £400 million on something they both agree is a good thing.

Nevertheless we should by no means write off the NFU: they are still a very efficient and powerful organisation, with immense resources available to them, particularly when you consider the contrast with the voluntary conservation bodies ranged against them. They have huge amounts of money, expert and effective staff. We may be winning the argument, but we are still a very long way from winning the fight to get legislation and policy changed or the flows of money altered in any significant way. You can get a lot of very powerful television programmes putting the conservation case but not get another £1 spent on conservation.

The last remark was particularly interesting, to say the least.

Lord Melchett continued to give first-class practical advice to anyone seeking to influence Parliament, concluding with the need to plug away, and saying: 'There is no point in swanning into Parliament on Monday and expecting to go home again on Tuesday afternoon and not go back for another 20 years'. How right!

Achieving Change

As Mr Mattingly also rightly says, it is much easier to defend the status quo than to achieve change. That is why the RA puts such effort into carefully checking proposals to alter rights of way, plough over footpaths, and so on. It means keeping steady contact with civil servants. It also means constantly reminding individual members to check what is happening in their locality or favoured spots and reporting any changes they believe to be imminent or that they see happening. The striking description adopted by the RA is 'damage limitation'.

The Association works with up to 100 other relevant organizations, not always in close harmony. When necessary, it forms or joins consortia to lobby for a case. It also recognizes the importance of the media, notably the early morning BBC *Today* programme, much listened to by MPs.

The NFU sees the protection of the countryside rather differently. It looks on itself as the most influential pressure group in Britain (even announcing it on its letterhead and some other printed material), owing some of its importance to the fact that its role was incorporated into the law in 1947. The other part of its importance naturally attaches to the fundamental position of the farming community. It also lays great stress on its expertise. It represents, it claims, the majority opinion of farmers. In the Ministry of Agriculture, Fisheries and Food it sees a mirror reflection of itself, matching with it skills of persuasion and argument exactly. Above all it wants farmers accepted as law-abiding citizens.

Apart from its probably unique role among pressure groups, the NFU relies on all the regular techniques. It keeps close and continual contact with civil servants (not only at the Agriculture Ministry), with MPs at all levels and of all parties, with agriculturally interested groups, and the media.

It would not be right to see the Ramblers' Association and the National Farmers Union as at daggers drawn. It would be right to see them as keeping an eye on each other, with Parliament and civil servants holding a watching brief, just in case. The interests of both are not identical but are not dissimilar.

What they have both discovered is one of the secrets of trying to exercise pressure. Persistence is the key. Legislation is introduced or altered for a variety of reasons, e.g. a clear need, a government desire, and pressure. The mechanics may bring the irresistible force (MPs wanting to be re-elected) face to face with the immovable object (the well known and sometimes justifiable Civil Service caution). To press for larger lorries or new motorways with the argument that this will bring down distribution costs and thus avoid more inflation has immediate appeal. It may run into delays while the Civil Service departments concerned ponder the effects on the road rebuilding programme, the noise pollution, the finances of the railways system, or other possibilities. But these are only factors of time. The situation is different for the nature societies who wish to preserve a site of special scientific interest. They have to marry two somewhat incompatible factors, lack of resources and persistence. The former is not insuperable, but only if there is a generous measure of the latter. However, it does take a pretty indomitable spirit. The greatest problems are faced by groups suddenly and without warning dragged into controversy. Pressure exercised through a trade association or professional body can create problems, if only because not all members may agree with a course of action and may express their disagreement publicly, allowing government to withstand the demands.

Opposition to Pressure

Pressure can sometimes succeed fairly quickly, particularly if it touches a widely held but not crystallized feeling. Quickly is still a relative term, since changes in legislation tend to happen in years rather than months. An idea may find its time but it may be long looking for it. The experience of abortion law reform will suffice. Bridget Pym, in her *Pressure Groups and the Permissive Society* (1974), showed how the Abortion Law Reform Association was founded in 1935 and campaigned until 1967, when the Abortion Act was passed. Of course, Mr Alton keeps it a live issue.

The British tendency to diffidence and suspicion of those who actively pursue a political solution to their objectives often leads to disapproval even from those who actually believe a cause is worthwhile. Auberon Waugh, the spiky commentator on the social scene, probably represented a sizeable percentage of the population when he wrote in *The Spectator*: ' . . . those unpleasant, strident, near hysterical pressure groups . . . which should be contradicted, put in their place and generally reviled whenever possible'.

He had support from a government minister, Douglas Hurd, who complained in a speech of the 'strangling serpents'' embrace of pressure groups. Mr Hurd argued that these groups distort the proper constitutional relation between the executive, Parliament, and the electorate. It would be too easy to dismiss this as the plaintive utterance of somebody whose cosy life was going to be disturbed by people asking questions or demanding that he hear their views. In fact it seemed more like a standard knee-jerk reaction from somebody who felt that his experience and position entitled him to believe he knew best and should not have to justify his position.

It drew an angry comment from a spokesman for the National Council of Voluntary Organisations, who claimed there was a distinction between special interest groups lobbying on behalf of the drugs industry, farming or car manufacturers, for example, and community pressure groups representing voices and causes which might not otherwise be heard. This was an equally suspect point of view. As Gertrude Stein might have said: 'A pressure group is a pressure group is a pressure group'. The NCVO spokesman was much nearer the mark when he pointed out that there were

> . . . some important questions to ask about pressure groups. How accountable are they to their supporters? How open are they in their methods? Do they sometimes rely too much on emotional appeal? Are all minority interests getting a fair hearing?

Incidentally, the answers to those questions are probably: as much as the supporters want to know, as much as they need to be, yes, and no. He came closest when he concluded:

> Of course, pressure groups make life difficult for government ministers. They put forward alternative, often conflicting points of view. They compete for attention. Ministers and government have to decide between them. But isn't this their job – listening to what the public has to say and then making decisions which *they* feel are in the public interest? Democracy is difficult but surely it is right.

Pressure Absorbed

Arguing that commercial pressure groups are bad and non-commercial ones are pure and holy is just ever so slightly specious.

Michael Moran's important reminder (*Politics and Society in Britain*) that many of the most powerful pressure groups 'are not separate from government; they are absorbed into the state, playing a large part in making and executing policy' raises an interesting issue. A pressure group may cease to be one when it loses its clear and radical identity. The moment that the ideas it advances become those of the orthodox establishment, it can be argued that it is no longer a pressure group. It is merely one other voice in preserving the steady roll forward of unadventurous policies dedicated to the lowest common denominator. In the words of one writer, it becomes 'sullied by compromise'. Saying that does not equal arguing for opposition for the sake of opposition. Governments have some of the best cards in their hand when it comes to stifling protest or reform, from setting up committees of enquiry to Royal Commissions and – perhaps the most deadly of all – embracing the opposition and suffocating it with kindness and agreement (at least on the surface).

The essential point is that pressure groups are necessary in a healthy, lively society. Their motives may be questioned but their existence cannot be.

In seeking to decide whether pressure is effective it does not specially matter whether the reference is to 'pressure' groups or 'interest' groups. They come to the same thing in the end. A pressure group is usually formed with the specific purpose of achieving legislative change. The Campaign for Freedom of Information may be taken as an example. An interest group could be a trade association or professional body which includes among its other objectives the monitoring of Parliament and keeping an eye on legislation that does or may affect its members. It can then decide whether to work within the legislation or to campaign to alter it.

Whether groups are classified as 'interest' or 'pressure', the tactics open to them are the same. They must look to direct contact with MPs and government departments and the indirect effect created by the media or by the publication of booklets, reports and surveys. The only real difference between them may well be the pace at which they operate. A genuine pressure group must try to get a result while what it is concerned with remains a public issue. Timing may also be critical. Approaching a general election, government and opposition parties are often hypersensitive to what they believe to be the groundswells of opinion, as noted both in their own research among their known supporters and in the published polls. They can be tempted to insert promises into manifestos, even when they actually have little intention of honouring them, or when they study them in detail find they are genuinely impractical. It is a time when the media may be specially useful to a pressure group.

The speed with which Parliament, the media, and most people become bored with the repetition of a subject or a cause can work against a group. Perversely, it can also sometimes work for them, but that is unusual. The cry 'Oh, no, not that again!' is a danger signal, especially for a limited subject. For instance, it is arguable that football hooliganism and the well meaning attempts of some groups to bring in legislation that would 'cure' it are doomed to failure. People are much more likely just to turn their backs on the game with a shrug of the shoulders than to agitate for reform. For a narrowly identified aim the majority in society has to 'care', and clearly the majority do not care enough about football gangs to want to do much about them.

Organizing Pressure

Turning an issue from bar gossip — 'We should do something about that' — into a movement that actually does do something about it demands organization. Either a single person or a small group has to set up a plan of action, allocate responsibilities, and above all maintain enthusiasm. Without these the group will fizzle out. That rule applies just as surely to campaigners on a real national issue as to a local group trying to get improved bus services.

There must also be a recognizable degree of altruism. Plain evidence of self-seeking makes success much more elusive, and also may make it more related to the amount of money available with which to support a campaign. Parliament and public may be unlikely to believe somebody who disclaims personal benefit from an advocated course of action, but they are still likely to give it a hearing. To maintain, as the NCVO spokesman seemed to, that because commercial companies profit from legislation they have sought to influence, they should be disbarred, is at the least naive. They may bring equal or greater benefit to society if they succeed. Above all, pressure groups must move with the times, by monitoring changes in attitude and shifts in the balance of power in society.

Any group has to remember that it exists in a society which contains other groups directly opposed to it, a society with certain accepted ways of doing things, and one growing ever more suspicious of motives. It is no longer enough to assume that 'I believe' said loudly enough will quickly cause everybody else to bow down three times and agree. Groups which have serious hopes of succeeding must know how far they can go in breaking the rules. It may be true that progress often means breaking the law but it can depend heavily on how it is broken. Overplaying the hand is a dangerous and usually unsuccessful tactic.

The original question still has to be answered. Does pressure work and is it worth the trouble? Studies throw up ambivalent attitudes.

Brenda Pym (*Pressure Groups and the Permissive Society*), writing in the early seventies, since when attitudes and standards have changed, was undecided. However, she seemed more or less certain that the 'radical' or 'moral' groups about which she was writing had little chance of success. She said:

> ... campaigns by radical groups have no hope of success while the government is hostile; even when unsuccessful they may be performing a useful role in keeping alive support among the opposition; conservative groups can maintain their position, given a favourable government, with relatively little effort; groups have little direct effect on the content of legislation, though their ideas may find their way independently into it; groups can do little to ensure the passage of a contentious Act, which is dependent upon the good offices of the government; groups opposed to reform can do relatively little in the face of a

determined government; and pressure groups may indirectly influence reform in that their ideas inform the basic predispositions of government.

She was somewhat hedging her bets, but that is no uncommon thing among commentators and writers on the political scene. Anthony H. Birch (in the 7th edition of his standard work, *The British System of Government*) noted that 'moral issues provide good opportunities for MPs acting on behalf of pressure groups, because governments are reluctant to insist on party discipline in such matters'. Later he maintained that public concern about the role of pressure groups 'seems to have little foundation'. As he said:

> There is as much freedom to organize pressure groups as there is to contest elections or form political parties. Wealth is not necessary to success and can never guarantee it. Money is always useful, but as a resource for a pressure group it appears to be less valuable than specialized information, enthusiasm, good contacts, the ability to get favourable publicity, and the power to hinder the administrative process by obstruction of one kind or another.

More general support came from Michael Moran, who wrote:

> Pressure groups are now the most obvious and important way in which communal interests and preferences influence what happens in the political arena. The importance of groups therefore lies only partly in their ability directly to intervene in politics; it lies also in their ability to control economic resources and to shape social values.

Then, in *Parties and Pressure Groups*, W. N. Coxall summed it all up by asserting: 'The claim that pressure groups exert excessive influence is therefore "not proven"'.

Pressure groups can succeed and are entirely necessary in a free society. But it may take a long time and a convergence of uncoordinated factors before a conclusion is reached. Wars can be won even when battles are lost.

6

HALF TIME –
NO SCORE DRAW

Some attempts at changing the law go rumbling on for years, even when 'the law is an ass'. Reform of the abortion laws took more than 50 years.

The simple expression of the rights and wrongs of a case is not the key. According to one writer, 'People don't like facts. They rely on their emotions'.

Sunday trading is a good example. The issue is a mixture of facts, emotions, the law and its observance or interpretation, local feelings, tradition and a host of other confusing factors. Early in 1986 the government decided not to proceed with an announced intention to allow Sunday trading, after a series of debates in the House of Lords and one debate in the Commons.

The right to open a shop on Sunday is undoubtedly a messy situation. In the atmosphere of the eighties, with a government dedicated to allowing free enterprise its head and retailers anxious to find any opportunity to increase their business, Sunday looked like the golden road. Here was the day when do-it-yourself fanatics and eager gardeners were in the right frame of mind. When so many families had both adults working through the week, Saturday was reserved for other activities, much of it as a heavy shopping day. Longer opening hours through the week were only part of the answer. It had to be Sunday. The existing law was open to several interpretations, and clearly was not entirely logical. Some English retailers especially in the DIY superstores looked enviously over the border to Scotland, where Sunday opening had been permissible since 1947. Society there did not seem to have collapsed into chaos, though many employees resented losing their Sundays.

Accordingly a number of retail outlets were opened, in defiance of the law. Local authorities, who had the responsibility for deciding whether to prosecute the offenders, seemed ambivalent. Some acted quickly to close the stores, others imposed nominal fines, and a third category did nothing about it.

It all looked like an interesting avenue for a government to wander down. The trick was to find a way of pleasing those who wanted the right to trade (thus adding their votes to the goodwill bank) without upsetting those who were against (thus losing their votes). One classic tactic in a situation like this is an enquiry of some sort. Royal Commissions and Select Committees are the grand way of doing this. Otherwise an ordinary committee under the chairmanship of somebody on the list of the great and the good is a handy method.

The background to Sunday trading goes back to dim history and, obviously, is securely and closely linked to observance of the Lord's Day. An Act in 1911 and another in 1936 'tidied up' the provisions of the law and created some confusing situations with which many people are familiar. What you can buy or not buy is a muddle, and even many smaller retailers are not too sure. In 1950 the subject was again considered and the result was the Shops Act, which is now the one that governs. Prompted by various interests, there have been eighteen attempts to abolish or reform the 1950 Act in the shape of Private Members' Bills. The pace of the attempts has hotted up in that thirteen of the eighteen were made between 1976 and 1983. The last one, in 1983, was introduced by Ray Whitney, the Conservative Member for Wycombe, after a Lords debate had shown a majority in favour of a change. It began to look even more like a smoke signal, so the Prime Minister announced that she agreed with those who wanted another enquiry. Earlier ones had been instituted by the Home Office (the sponsoring ministry) but its recommendations had been shelved. It took another 6 months before the Auld committee (led by Mr Robin Auld, QC) was appointed. It was charged with the task of examining what changes were needed and to recommend how they might be achieved. The terms of appointment also made it clear that the committee was to keep in mind the interests of customers and workers, as well as the 'traditional character' of Sunday.

Government Support

The committee submitted its recommendations in October 1984, and they were published in the following month. In the interval they had taken written evidence from 300 interested parties and more than 7,000 individuals, and had interviewed representatives of eleven organizations.

The committee was unanimous in recommending the abolition of all restrictions on Sunday trading hours, with some qualifications as to the protection of employees. In December 118 Members signed an Early Day Motion welcoming the report, and a short while after another similar move attracted another 104 names. The Home Secretary was publicly pleased with the committee.

The government acted in May 1985, when the full weight of the Prime Minister, supported by the Foreign Secretary, the Home Secretary, the Chancellor and the Secretaries of State for Scotland and Wales was lined up behind a motion accepting the report and asking the government to introduce legislation. The House acquiesced, with a majority of 120 in favour, though the debate was heated. The government may not have noticed the members of its own party who abstained or voted against, or may have decided that it had enough firepower to discount internal opposition.

It must all have looked like a relatively easy path to popularity, so the government went ahead. It chose to introduce the very short Shops Bill – with schedules and consequential amendments to existing law it only ran to nine pages – in the House of Lords. This was interpreted as an indication that, while the government was anxious to court favour by bowing to alleged public

67

demand, it actually was quite prepared for the bill to be thrown out. This would have left the government with its hands clean and a good measure of injured innocence ('they' appeared to want it, 'we' offered it to them and 'they' changed their minds). However, the bill's purpose was 'to remove certain restrictions as to the opening hours of shops and other places where a retail trade or business is carried on and the working hours of adults employed in them; to make transitional provision as to the rights of persons so employed concerning Sunday working; and for connected purposes'.

It had its formal introduction on 14 November 1985, and moved to the second reading on 2 December. The debate on the second reading subsequently occupied 27½ hours on that day and four others.

Support Outside Parliament

Outside Parliament the forces in favour of the bill were led by the Federation of Multiple DIY Retailers, comprising the nine major companies in the field, covering 50 per cent of the market, 500 outlets, and more than 30,000 employees. They were supported by the National Consumer Council and the Consumers' Association. They had been lobbying actively and persistently for several years. They had powerful evidence to present, the result of surveys undertaken both by the NCC and the Federation itself. All, it was said, showed that a majority of individuals wanted a change in the law to allow more freedom to retailers. The individuals questioned included both customers and shop workers. The Federation stated that Sunday trading would lead to lower prices since it allowed a bigger spread of overheads; would produce more jobs (a point of especial appeal to the government); would not lead to 7-day working for employees, who would be on a rota that gave them 2 days off each week; and would not herald the end of the small corner shop. It also claimed that religious observance would not be affected. All in all, the agents for change – backed by a strong media operation and a highly professional lobbying consultancy – wondered how they could they lose a campaign which they had been assiduously conducting since 1950.

The Opposition

Michael Windridge, then director of Government affairs, The McCann Consultancy, described how the opposition had been hastily marshalled, in a speech he gave to the Institute of Public Relations conference in October 1986. He introduced his review of how the bill was defeated by reminding his audience that 'he who has not the ear of the Member of Parliament's secretary will serve no great political cause with any notable distinction. The MP's secretary – the arbiter, quite literally, of what correspondence and circulars do or do not go into the waste bin – was a key target figure in our Parliamentary campaign'. One of them complained at lunch with Mr Windridge one day of the 'vast amount of mail her Member was receiving from irate constituents on the subject of Sunday trading'.

Mr Windridge then went into some of the details of the campaign his consultancy had mounted.

'It was everywhere assumed that the Bill would receive safe legislative passage, with only a few parliamentary waves expected to be created by the bench of bothersome bishops in the House of Lords. Two members of my immediate family still work a 6 day week as directors of a small family retail business in Wolverhampton. It was the declared intention of one of their principal chain store competitors to open on Sundays if the Bill became law. Like thousands of other small business owners at the time, they felt *they also* would be obliged to open on Sundays as well, in order to protect market-share.

'A week later, through a chance telephone call to the Jubilee Centre in Cambridge, a small research organization which was to play eventually the key organizational role in the campaign, I was invited to sit in, as observer, on a steering committee meeting of the Keep Sunday Special coalition, as it then called itself. There, to my dismay and frustration as the meeting progressed, sat the massed ranks of the representatives of both God *and* Mammon, waging – it seemed to me – a pretty futile holy communications' war against the proposed Bill. Representing the Ranks of Mammon and the Retail Industry sat the general secretary of the Federation of Master Butchers, at that stage with his meat hook (metaphorically speaking) firmly embedded in the representative of the Lord's Day Observance Society sitting opposite. On his left scowled the Parliamentary officer of the Co-operative Union. With a retail turnover exceeding £4.5 billion, some 8 million members, and 5,800 retail outlets, employing over 100,000 workers the Co-op needed no sermonising from the assistant secretary of the Catholic Bishops conference, who sat dejectedly beside him. Also there, the Multiple Shoe Retailers Association, representing 70 per cent of the leading high street shoe shops.

'They'd got the boot, so to speak, into the Director General of the National Chamber of Trade, he a hardened campaigner with many shops bills battles behind him, speaking on behalf of the Chambers' 200,000 affiliated smaller size businesses.

'Also in communion with their fellow members around that boardroom steering committee were: The British Council of Churches, the Church of England Board of Social Responsibility, and the Evangelical Alliance. I was going to add the Boy Scouts, the Salvation Army, the Girl Guides, the Mothers' Union and even the Shop Workers' Union USDAW but – much relief – it was only later that all these organisations indicated their willingness to come on board the campaign. Last, but not least, the British Hardware Federation, representing well over a thousand of the smaller hardware and ironmongers shops who feared that many of their members could face possible extinction.

'However, we knew them to be a fantastic crowd of people all totally committed to a cause in which they passionately believed, and all of whom had worked tirelessly within their own organisations and trade associations to campaign against the Government's proposals.

'The trouble was, and they were the first to recognise it, their case was clearly going by default. They had made negligible combined impact on the press and on public and parliamentary opinion. The Bill was due to be introduced in the Lords in three weeks' time, and we advised that unless an immediate remedial communications' strategy was adopted, their battle was lost.

Marshalling the Campaign

'The retailers' argument could be summarized as follows: they didn't want the Bill, there was no manifesto commitment for such a contentious measure, and they didn't believe their customers wanted it. They knew for certain their staff didn't want it. In the main, the only retailers who did want it were, naturally enough, the DIY super-stores and the garden centres. It was our primary objective therefore to expose the widely held myth that retailers were all crying out in unison for the end to all regulations on Sunday trading. The true facts told a different story: the Auld Committee report itself admitted, and I quote "it would however be misleading to leave the impression that there is an incessant general clamour for Sunday shopping . . ." The same Auld report quoted The Retail Consortium, which stated categorically that "the majority of the trade was strongly in favour of maintaining some control of trading hours on Sundays". The report continued: "Most of the big shop names of the High Street favour regulation, particularly of Sunday trading. They include the Co-operative movement, the House of Fraser, the John Lewis Partnership, Marks and Spencer and most of the big food chains, including Safeway and Sainsbury's . . ." It went on: "Other familiar names in favour of regulation in one form or another are Argos, Bejam, Budgen, Ketts, Radio Rentals, Sears Holdings (which includes Selfridges) and Timpsons".

'Why on earth, we asked ourselves, with all that degree of opposition, hadn't the leading retailers themselves taken the initiative and worked together to campaign against the Bill at a much earlier stage? The simple fact of the matter was: they had collectively assumed the matter to be a *fait accompli* and with the size of the Government's majority they might as well resign themselves to preparing their stores for seven days a week trading. We had a devil of a job convincing them that if only all the major retailers opposed to the measure would actually publicly say so, our campaign would be greatly strengthened.

'A similar political fatalism had, in my own view, struck the mainstream churches by that stage. The churches' case can be summarized as follows: that Christians believe that Sunday should be preserved as a distinctive and special day – that it is not right for Christians to seek to impose their views on others who don't share their belief, that is not God's way – but when they believe that a Christian position embodies something which reflects a fundamental need for men and women, and for society, they have a duty to try to persuade others. That in addition to its Christian meaning and significance, the observance of Sunday as a day different from the rest reflects a basic need for individuals and society to have a rhythm of life which is recognised as a day primarily set apart for rest, recreation, leisure and, for some, worship.

'Throughout the campaign, we encouraged the church to emphasise more emphatically the Christian understanding of Sunday as traditionally positive and life affirming and family affirming. It was not to be a day identified with a negative and restricted sabbatarianism.

'Of course it was going to suit the Government if the principal objections to the Bill were seen to be coming from the church, rather than from the retail sector and from shop workers themselves. Perhaps that is why the Bill started off life in the Lords – the bothersome bishops would be expected to mount a strong attack on the Bill's provisions, but, so ministers must have calculated, they would be unlikely to rally great support to their cause. One cabinet minister had indeed suggested to the press that, as a group, the bishops were not particularly popular with the other parties. He was reported to have said, I quote, "They pontificate and then go away, and this does not seem to endear them to other peers".

'So naturally it was our primary objective to ensure that the campaign was seen visibly to be led by the retailers, shop workers and sympathetic MPs of all parties. We deliberately timed the press launching of our campaign after the Bill had been introduced in the Lords. The campaign was not against Sunday trading. It supported the Government in its wish to tidy up the anomalies of the Shops Acts, but it was not in favour of total de-regulation of trading restrictions on Sunday.

'Our aim was to increase public and parliamentary awareness of the consequences of the new Bill, and to argue that the Government had acted too hastily in presenting a Bill which, because it hadn't appeared in the manifesto, had not had the qualified support of a fraction of even the Conservative voting equipment – a Bill which had been introduced, in other words, without adequate consultation and safeguards.

Finding Allies

'Firstly, we encouraged the formation of a new campaign organisation, which was the obvious evolutionary development from the 'keep Sunday special coalition'. We called it 'the keep Sunday special campaign'. We appointed a chairman, a director general, a research director, and a press officer. We assembled a list of patrons from the great and the good of the land, representing all the major churches, retail and political interest groups. The campaign steering committee continued to meet on a weekly basis, every Friday morning.

'At this stage the union of shop workers – USDAW – were not yet officially part of the campaign organisation. We were obviously an unknown and untried entity and they were actually cautious about identifying themselves with us too closely at that stage.

'So in spite of much behind the scenes diplomatic activity, we failed to persuade them to appear at the press conference table working together with us. However, we did manage to persuade the general secretary to send us a letter of endorsement for our campaign – we therefore were able to enclose a copy of the

USDAW statement of support in all the press packs we issued at the conference.

'But perhaps of even greater diplomatic and publicity value was the signed declaration of support for the campaign from the three church leaders, namely: the Archbishop of Canterbury, the Catholic leader, Basil Hume, and the moderator of the Free Church Council representing the Methodists, Baptists, Presbyterians etc. We enclosed these letters in our press pack, which we also sent on to every Member of Parliament.

'As I have emphasised earlier, we wanted to ensure that the campaign was not seen as a negative, sabbatarian collection of kill-joys, but rather a body of people representing widely-differing organisations but with a common concern at the possible effect the Bill would have on the family life of small-sized retailers and their staff as well as families of larger shops and stores.

'So we asked the President of the Mothers' Union to launch the parliamentary campaign by releasing 650 balloons in Parliament Square, one for each parliamentary constituency. In addition, we wanted to demonstrate that we were a fun-loving family life affirming campaign so we involved our friends, the Federation of Meat Traders, in a publicity stunt.

'As a symbol of the family Sunday, they delivered a huge joint of the best Scotch beef to No 10 Downing Street – enough to provide a cut for each member of the Cabinet. The campaign also delivered individual joints to each of the opposition leaders, and to each member of the press who attended our press conference.

'We eagerly awaited our inevitable massive press coverage the following day. Sure enough it was reported not only on the front pages of every national daily, but also on the back pages and pages 2 and 3 as well. The previous day's event at Downing Street had pushed every other news item to one side. The motto: always check before you hold a press conference whether it is the intention of the Secretary of State for Defence (Michael Heseltine) to throw a resignation tantrum in Cabinet on the same day!

This exposition of the attack on the Bill shows how it may be necessary in a successful campaign to use tactics as different as carefully reasoned arguments and stunt publicity. However, it also reinforces the point made elsewhere in this book: it is almost certainly easier to preserve the status quo than to change it.

When Lord Glenarthur, Parliamentary Under Secretary of State at the Home Office, moved the second reading of the bill he called it 'a liberalising but steady reforming measure to rescue the law from the disrepute into which it has fallen. The aim', he continued 'is to bring the law into line with the realities of life, tastes and behaviour in the late twentieth century, and to extend individual choice'.

Perhaps what the government and the proponents of the bill had missed was highlighted by Lord Brougham and Vaux, when he remarked that it was 'another of those issues where not entirely but by and large the forces of passion are ranged against those of reason'. The present Sunday trading law is a hotch-potch, but as one campaigner for the change noted rather sadly, 'Nasty things, facts – people don't like them'.

Throughout the 5 days of debate on the second reading (not continous debate, since it was interrupted from time to time by urgent other matters) most of the speeches were predictable, but it became steadily clearer and clearer that a head of steam likely to blow the bill into oblivion was building up. The same thing happened when the bill went to report. A further 9 hours of debate at that stage was followed by another hour on the third reading. Between the beginning of December and the end of February the Lords had applied their minds to the issue and were obviously not in favour.

Wrong Assumptions

The closing battle was in the Commons on 14 April, when the Home Secretary was interrupted several times as he spoke to the bill. The arguing went on from 3.45 to midnight. At the end of it John Biffen, the leader of the House, was forced to concede that the temper of the House was such that no further progress could be made, and that the 'Government has no plans to reintroduce the legislation'.

But it is *au revoir* and not goodbye to a sensible set of decisions of what should be allowed or not allowed on Sundays.

To some extent the Government miscalculated the strength of the opposition and the backbench revolt. It was difficult for the proponents to maintain a high level of media interest, but rather easier for the opponents to do so. Now the opponents of any change need do nothing very much, though they have announced proposals to try to tidy up the situation. It is in their interest to let the subject die, and in that they will have the passive support of the media. The only time any press interest will be evinced is if one of the major multiples decides to stage an all-out rebellion and open all its outlets to see what happens. That is an unlikely scenario, since the fines would now be much heavier and the press interest would evaporate fairly quickly.

Meanwhile the supporters have a different task. They have to beaver away at trying to keep the issue live. They have already made some moves. While realizing that some potential allies might not be the most useful to have on board, they have widened their base. They have undertaken some very limited advertising under the aegis of the 'Committee to Sort Out Sunday', in which they urged 'all members of the public who agree please write to your local MP now'. They have drafted a bill for introduction by a backbench MP, though the Government has said that it will study the subject again – in due course. They have to try to get a commitment to the principle from the opposition parties, just in case the government changes next time round. At the same time they accept that it is probably unlikely that the issue can be effectively raised for another 2–3 years. Most present MPs will probably play 'wait and see'.

This lengthy case history illustrates a number of key points about lobbying. Timing is critical. The luck may run away from you. The great English characteristics of tradition and hypocrisy may turn a whole question upside down, favourably or otherwise; as Bernard Shaw well called one of his plays, *You Never Can Tell*. Sunday trading, freedom of information, the Channel Tunnel, and a host of others are all subjects which will come back and back. The lesson for those devotedly attached to a cause has to be: 'If at first you don't succeed; Try, try again'.

7

YOU WIN SOME –
YOU LOSE SOME

Although widely practised and acknowledged as an acceptable business tool, lobbying remains a fairly secretive affair. It is not surprising. Parliament, and especially government, does not care to admit too easily that it has bent to pressure. Pressure groups do not care to boast too readily of their successes, for fear that Parliament (and, even more, Whitehall) will seek revenge at some later date. Equally obviously they will not trumpet their failures.

For those reasons case histories are not always easy to come by. However, when published or revealed in some other way, they all show the same elements: meticulous preparation, reasoned briefing, careful choice of both allies and the aspects of legislation on which to stand and fight, well judged use of all the available resources and techniques, and – perhaps above all – time.

Peter Luff, managing director of Good Relations Public Affairs, put it well when he was explaining his firm's role in a battle to persuade government not to issue regulations banning a product made by one of his clients. He said:

The essence of public affairs is good communication conducted over a long period of time to create an atmosphere of understanding for your case. The political world is a complex maze and that simple task of effective communication is correspondingly difficult. Lobbying is a much-abused word and lobbyists a much-abused breed. If you push me into a corner I will admit to being a lobbyist, but only under duress. I suppose this is because of accusations about private conspiracies against the public interest. All the issues my company deals with – many of them very sensitive – must be capable of being discussed publicly. Indeed they will sometimes only be resolved satisfactorily if they are discussed publicly. The Commons Select Commitee on Members' Interests re-affirmed the right of the citizen to lobby his MP and to use professional assistance if he thought that would better advance his case. So what is the objective of the use of public affairs consultants? In essence I believe it is to create an environment in which a particular decision is the easy one to take. This can only be done if the case itself is sustainable and respectable. Often the challenge for the consultant is to define the message and to make sure it is acceptable to a political audience.

No lobbyist can make black white or white black – but there are generally shades of grey.

However, a large part of the public affairs consultant's income derives not from sustained communications planned and organised over three-year periods to precise timetables and budgets. Sadly, much of it comes from helping businesses to resolve short-term crises.

The absolute need for time, particularly when an industry is concerned with widely held impressions of it rather than with trying to introduce or alter a specific piece of legislation, is reinforced in the following brief study.

Oysters and Paint

As Peter Luff noted, the consultant is often called in at the eleventh hour to try to solve a crisis which might have been foreseen or which equally might have erupted unexpectedly. In his case it was 'the sad and puzzling story of a company whose product one year won the Queen's Award for Export Achievement – and the next was going to be banned for poisoning oysters'.

The situation brought into conflict a well established, highly reputable manufacturer, International Paint, and a group of oyster farmers in the West Country. The yacht paint business is a very small and specialized market served with a range of decorative and marine products. A vital part of it is anti-fouling, applied to boats kept afloat for extended periods to protect the hulls from infestation by marine growth. When International Paint started supplying yacht anti-fouling in 1934, the products were formulated on cuprous oxide liberally laced with arsenic or mercury. Up to 1970 cuprous oxide remained the most important active ingredient, boosted by various other biocides. Then a new and much more effective biocide, tributyl tin oxide (TBT), became available. It could be used as a booster, or, mixed as an additive into a resin, used as the main ingredient in its own right. From then and into the early 1980s TBT was the backbone of International Paints' worldwide sales of yacht anti-foulings. They became known as 'free association paints', which work by the TBT slowly leaching out of the paint over several months. In this quality they exhibited one main disadvantage: they are very wasteful of TBT in the first few weeks. TBT is very expensive – at the time of this case the cost was about £9,500 a ton – so that chemists sought an alternative. In 1978 they succeeded and launched the first copolymer yacht anti-fouling, in which the TBT is reacted to form a methacrylate so that the entire paint film is active. One major advantage was that the emission of TBT into the water is reduced about 80 per cent.

The company won the Queen's Award for Technology for the development and global marketing. At first the copolymer was expensive, but by 1984 it became possible to produce it in a medium price bracket. The 'improved' paint was launched in January 1984 – and ran into trouble in 6 weeks.

First signs were from the media in the West Country, where the headlines 'Killer paint should be banned' began to appear. It stemmed from a campaign started by a small group of oyster farmers in the region, based on work published in the Ministry of Agriculture, Fisheries and Food *Water Pollution Bulletin*. International Paints called in Good Relations, which immediately raised a number of queries. Was the ministry's evidence sound, what was the statistical evidence, had there been laboratory experiments to prove effects in a natural environment, and why had the ministry become so concerned? In addition, who were the oyster farmers, what were their problems, and could they be solved by other means than simply banning the International Paints' product? What attitude would be taken by the Department of the Environment, did it understand how long it might take the manufacturer to adapt his product, and how were the government likely to react? Lastly, how was the press campaign to be combated?

It rapidly became clear that the government was going down the simple avenue – a virtual complete ban on TBT, which would affect almost every yacht anti-fouling made in Britain. Manufacturers, including International Paints, had already been invited to formal discussions with the Department of the Environment, but ministers were saying both publicly and privately that TBT was going to be banned.

The consultancy set about looking for answers to a number of questions. Were there sound arguments the industry could present, was its case genuinely in the public interest, was there an environmentally acceptable alternative, and for that matter was there any alternative the government could agree to?

Having satisfied itself that there were proper answers to all these questions, the consultancy was able to work out a plan of campaign. Put simply, it began with trying to seek a private solution to avoid wasting both the government's and the industry's time on a massive public squabble. If that failed, there would have to be recourse to a public campaign, lasting throughout the statutory consultation period.

From the company's point of view the whole operation was immensely time-consuming. International's Peter Blackman spent about 80 per cent of his time dealing with the problem, for almost 12 months, while the company's marine biologists were tied up for about half their time. The company's strengths in putting over its case were its knowledge of the market, its own products, the needs of the user, paint technology and marine biology. It was (and is) a well known company which believed it was trusted in the market. What it did not know was much about the oyster growers. The campaign therefore included early discussions with them. Having done that, International became convinced that they could grow oysters where the farmers were alleging that the anti-fouling was poisoning their stocks. They set up an oyster-growing experiment.

But in the world of Parliament and Whitehall International were the innocents abroad. They needed to find out how to make presentations to civil servants and to Parliament, how to draft documents that would be acceptable, how to time their campaign, and how to co-ordinate their activities with those of other manufacturers. It was for those special skills they called in the consultancy.

The government appeared to have made up its mind, without much comprehension of the consequences of its actions. Rational argument failed. The government announced that it was going to issue regulations under the Control of Pollution Act 1974. Examination of them led International to point out that they were grossly discriminatory between yachtsmen, allowed no time for the industry to develop environmentally acceptable alternatives, and threatened even greater environmental damage than TBT was alleged to cause.

The consultancy turned to its potentially greatest ally. Said Peter Luff:

The yachting community is like a juggernaut – hard to get rolling but once going almost unstoppable. A handful of oystermen had exerted a lot of pressure. We decided to see what a couple of hundred thousand yachtsmen could do during the 90 day consultation period given to us.

Together we organised a media campaign, produced a leaflet and poster and put them into as wide a circulation as possible, stating our case and asking yachtsmen to write to the DoE objecting to the proposed regulations. We faced the media. All public appearances were made by International Paints personnel, but only three people in the company made public statements. We never refused to make an appearance or make on the record comments to the media. Liaison with MPs was taken on by the company. Continuing liaison was maintained with the two principal 'third parties' – the Ship & Boat Builders National Federation and the Royal Yachting Association.

Our task was made difficult when the government suddenly introduced new evidence and new claims in the middle of the consultation period.

Ministers did not like the tone we had adopted and said so in letters to their constituents, but more than 1,000 representations from ordinary yachtsmen to the DoE proved irresistible. The Department started off sending statements defending their position, and ended up sending simple acknowledgements. MPs, led by the RYA, made their feelings clear. Even the oystermen said the proposals were more draconian than they wanted.

Lead Time

The government had another look, and the result was a new set of regulations which met environmental, user and industry needs. In fact they were the very regulations that industry proposed at the beginning. They were not perfect but there was time for everyone to work out a sensible solution. There was to be no immediate ban on TBT and more research was to be undertaken. It was a package everyone could accept.

For the company it represented an agreement which it would have accepted at the outset, but, more importantly, protection of a major international market while more satisfactory alternatives were developed. There would be no explosion of untried alternatives, no divisions between owners of large yachts and owners of small ones, and effective anti-fouling paints would still be available.

For the oysters there was the prospect of reduced TBT levels in the short term and a long-term ban if it proved necessary.

The basic point of the operation was that all sides had learnt about each other's problems, so that future regulations could be drafted from a base of better background knowledge. It created an 'amicable talking shop' which was getting things done, rather than a legislative nightmare.

For the consultancy it proved again that, for a company operating in a sensitive market, communication with the political world is needed all the time. If a problem appears, however distantly on the horizon, companies should start talking to government as soon as possible and certainly before minds are made up. In Peter Luff's own words:

Do not rely on making your case alone. Try to involve others. Third party endorsement never did any harm. Get close to the opposition. Remember that you can never be sure which of your actions is the decisive one that wins an argument, but a large volume of support always helps. Remember, too, that a complex issue is only ever understood by a handful of people – and never assume they understand it properly. A complex issue is likely to demand a complex solution and involve many valid alternative points of view.

If government is planning to do something you do not like, it is not necessarily being malicious. It could just be short of information. At the same time, people in government generally want to hear from the horse itself, not from its trainer. In situations like that faced by International, and indeed in any issue where Parliament and Whitehall are concerned, do not just turn to the company lawyer to handle a legislative problem. Public affairs advice and action may be the real answer.

It is right to end this revealing story by noting that TBT was eventually banned, but only after the industry had been given time and opportunity to find an acceptable alternative.

Bad Cars?

The automotive industry at the end of the 1970s was an industry under siege. Its products were poorly regarded, production levels were dropping and productivity was appalling. The industry was a by-word for the 'British Disease' – its industrial relations record was a national joke. And gathering momentum all the time was the Japanese invasion, as well as a developing challenge from the newly industrializing countries of the Far East. The British industry, vital if only because of the jobs and indeed communities it supported, was once second only to the United States, but was apparently in irreversible decline.

In this situation tough action was needed from management and workforce alike. Together the problems were tackled and the industry rapidly set its house in order. The products were improved, productivity gains matched those of competitors, there was massive investment in new technology, as well as in design and manufacture. Labour relations improved beyond all recognition. The motor industry was becoming more efficient, more dynamic, and above all more competitive. It was no longer a sunset industry, but a sunrise one. Ten years later this remains substantially true, despite the penetration of imported cars.

However, in the particular circumstances of the turn of the decade the reality of the industry's advance was tarnished by an outdated image – the old perceptions were still there. Britain still had the lowest level of car ownership in Europe. The industry was aggressively pursuing its target of 2 million new vehicles a year, but was hindered by an unfavourable fiscal regime. Cars were the only consumer durable to suffer tax on sales over and above VAT, and were the only item not VAT-deductible when used for business purposes. The industry needed a more favourable climate in which to grow, but the way in which it was regarded by those who could influence change was hampering attempts to change the conditions.

Government had to be convinced that the industry was vitally important to the nation's future. An understanding of the modern industry and the way it was responding to the challenges facing it had to be created among those able to influence the decisions which affected the climate in which it operated. They had to be convinced that the industry was worth encouraging.

Through its trade association, the Society of Motor Manufacturers and Traders, the industry identified the need for a long-term, structured programme to change the attitudes and remove the barriers to growth that were encountered as a result. The campaign was devised and supervised by McAvoy, Wreford Bayley. The ultimate target was government, but a number of different approaches – direct, indirect, and supportive – were used.

Traditionally the industry had well defined but limited channels through to government. These were to be refined and improved. At the same time they had to be widened to get into all departments that influenced decisions affecting the industry. Discussions on specific issues in regular contacts with ministers and their advisers were backed by additional background briefings. The same material began to be passed to ministers in other departments. Briefing material included documents on the current state of the industry and on particular issues such as the special car sales tax. Other means of keeping ministers informed were by encouraging backbench MPs to bring to ministers' attention motor industry issues in their constituencies.

Officials are an integral and vital part of government. Briefing them was a critical part of the programme. Again it was decided to broaden the approach beyond the traditional points of contact. Seminars were held for senior civil servants who had been charged with formulating advice to ministers. Seminar topics included the current state of the industry, together with more specific analysis of topics of particular interest to officials. The speakers included academics and senior managers from the industry. The contacts made at these seminars were augmented by regular mailed briefing notes.

MPs who had strong motor industry interests were already part of a group which received regular information. The number was, however, quite small, considering the size and importance of the industry. As it was represented and provided jobs to some degree in almost every constituency it was vital that links with as many members as possible were significantly strengthened.

Direct contact was made by mail with all MPs, and briefings on specific issues were organized. Communication was encouraged, so that they would seek information from the industry when taking part in relevant debates or raising questions. Early Day Motions were also used to generate interest on particular topics.

MPs also take note of issues which may affect their constituents, so senior executives in companies were encouraged to make contact with their local MP. In this way MPs could receive valuable information on how the government's policies were affecting individual companies in the industry. Although background information and briefing were provided for company executives, and seminars held to focus on how Parliament and government worked and how to communicate effectively with MPs, individuals were encouraged to present the industry's case in their own way.

The presentation of the case to politicians was not carried out in isolation. Complementary programmes were organized in other audience areas which might have some influence on the primary decision-makers. These included the media, trade unions, other business organizations, local government and the local community.

Where attitudes are already hardened to a considerable extent it takes time to change them. The programme to improve the image of the motor industry has proved no exception. It was seen at the outset as a long-term effort, and so far has been successful in moving opinion among politicians, other opinion formers and the general public to more favourable levels. Individual issues remain to be won, but success is more likely against a background of greater – and more supportive – understanding.

This could be taken as the story of a large and realistic industry attempting to alter the atmosphere in which it conducted its business. It had the resources to undertake such a wide-ranging campaign, and could see that the results were not easily quantifiable or identifiable. Car tax has not been removed, but that was probably less a genuine objective than a peg on which to hang introductory conversations.

Freezing Tobacco Tax

A shorter-term campaign was one to persuade the Chancellor of the Exchequer not to increase the taxes on tobacco. It was put together and carried out by the public affairs division of Daniel J. Edelman Ltd.

Any public affairs programme designed to affect the March Budget has a target audience of ultimately only one person – the Chancellor of the Exchequer. He receives submissions from many industries and interest groups with clear vested interests, whose cases can often suffer from the prejudice this can create, whatever the strength of the argument.

The campaign put together by Edelman had clear objectives:

– to politicize the issue of tobacco tax;
– to present strong, factual arguments in favour of a tax freeze and deliver them forcefully to identified political and media targets;
– to extend awareness of the arguments among politicians, gaining acceptance even among the industry's Parliamentary critics;
– to achieve significant third-party endorsement; and
– to generate widespread, sympathetic local media coverage to reinforce politicians' support.

The tobacco industry has been hard hit by tax increases consistently above the level of inflation. A third of the UK market has gone in the last decade, principally due to severe Budgets, and thousands of direct manufacturing jobs have been lost as a result. Other sectors have suffered, too: research shows that each direct job supports a further six or seven jobs in distribution, marketing and retailing.

Both tobacco manufacturers' and retailers' businesses therefore are badly affected by high tobacco tax rises. Given prevailing views on tobacco use, arguments against Budget increases are necessarily complex and not immediately acceptable to the layman – or backbench MP.

The Tobacco Alliance, established in 1983 as a communications network for the tobacco family and its allies, exists to bring together people whose livelihoods depend upon tobacco. A major and continuing theme of the Alliance is putting the case for fair treatment on tobacco tax. In autumn 1986 'Face the Facts, Freeze the Tax' set out to let the facts speak for themselves in support of a plea not to increase taxes. It was decided to deliver the arguments to individual constituency Members, for transmission to government via the medium of third-party industry supporters – tobacco retailers, primarily small independents.

The case which retailers could put strongly, and which would most appeal to MPs, was:

– the tax structure favours cheap foreign imported cigarettes, mainly found in big supermarkets and multiples. This endangers jobs in the independent retail sector as well as in manufacturing.
– independent retailers depend on tobacco not only for profits but also as a traffic-builder. The local amenity they provide is an important social service;
– tobacco-tax increases fuel inflation. An 11p increase (in the 1986 Budget) put almost two points on inflation; and
  – more tax would prevent an open Common Market, as the widely disparate rates of tobacco tax around Europe have to be harmonized before the EEC policy to end customs barriers can be realized.

Retailers Step In

The arguments were refined and distilled. They formed the backbone of an 8-minute video and accompanying 'manifesto' booklet, designed for viewing and reading by MPs. They were to be presented in person by a retailer to his own constituency MP. The 250 MPs targeted, spread all over the country, were selected because of constituency tobacco interest, Ministerial or Opposition rank, House or party committee office, or small electoral majorities.

Contact between retailers and MPs was organized in two phases. First came autumn constituency-based activity, and second a lobby of MPs at the House of Commons in February 1987. Successful operations hinged upon meticulous co-ordination of activity and timing, to ensure simultaneous development of the campaign in each of the ten regions. Liaison executives in the headquarters office maintained day-to-day contact with executives in the regions, who in turn dealt directly with retailers. Many retailers had taken part in previous exercises and agreed to take part again. Others were recruited through trade and trade association links. In some cases, where the MP and his constituency were judged to be critical, cold calls were made by regional offices, with a high level of success. Two hundred and fifty retailers, covering over a third of the Commons, were recruited. This activity took place in October, November and December 1986.

Guided by a comprehensive action manual (which included fact and argument briefing, schedule of activity, and specimen letters) retailers contacted their MPs, inviting them to their shops to view the video and to talk about the impact of tobacco tax. Where this was not possible, retailers met MPs at constituency surgeries, showing them the video on portable playback equipment. Where no meeting was possible, retailers sent the video and booklet by mail. Each regional office publicized these meetings with local news releases and photocalls. This phase of the campaign logged 136 personal meetings, 144 contacts by mail, and extensive local media coverage.

To reinforce the message and encourage further activity by MPs immediately pre-Budget, retailers were brought to London for a mass lobby. Through the support of a sponsoring MP, the Members' Dining Room was used for an afternoon reception, when 140 retailers from all over the country came to meet the 83 members who had previously confirmed their attendance. Many MPs congratulated their constituents on a successful and well organized lobby.

Again the media were addressed. This time a photocall was organized at Lambeth Pier opposite the Palace of Westminster: not only a shot of massed retailers, but 32 separate local media groupings. Planning the exercise necessitated readying captions for prints in advance and marshalling the subjects to stand in the right order. The half-hour session allowed only 2 minutes per shot and ended in time for retailers to pass through security into the House and their 4.00 pm meeting with MPs. Photographs were in the post to local media that afternoon and achieved additional press and radio coverage, bringing campaign airtime to more than one hour. The events of the afternoon were filmed for the record.

The campaign achieved its operational objectives: the tobacco-tax arguments reached and received impressive recognition by many Parliamentarians by way of hundreds of third parties. The Treasury and other ministers were in no doubt of the strength of feeling among small retailers, the substance of the arguments, and their endorsement by individual MPs. The campaign inspired many questions as well as signatories to an Early Day Motion on cheap foreign imported cigarettes. Media coverage was widespread, supportive, and – unusually on a tobacco issue – wholly factual and sympathetic.

Waste Disposal

The government first announced plans for the disposal of radioactive waste in October 1983. Two sites were investigated for their suitability for low and intermediate level radioactive waste disposal. They were Elstow in Bedfordshire for a shallow trench and Billingham in Cleveland for a deep repository. In January 1985 the Billingham site was abandoned and it was decided that at least two other sites for shallow trenches should be nominated.

In February 1986 three additional sites for exploration by NIREX, the disposal authority, were identified. The four sites were:

- Elstow in Bedfordshire
- Killingholme in Humberside
- Fulbeck in Lincolnshire
- Bradwell in Essex

Understandably the government announcement, caused wide-spread concern in the areas selected. Local community feeling expressed itself in the customary ways – petitions of protest, picketing of sites, widespread rallying of support.

All these actions were generally supported by the local authorities concerned. In Humberside, for example, the council employed a touring caravan to explain the basis of its alarm, and provide suitable campaign literature, car stickers and the rest. It also produced a video for presentation to MPs and peers before debates in Parliament as well as locally. Bedfordshire liaised with local pressure groups to issue a monthly newsletter, aimed at sustaining the protest. The three counties (Bedfordshire, Humberside and Lincolnshire) gave political and, in some cases, financial support to local protesters, who adopted memorable names – BAND, HAND and LAND (AND = Against Nuclear Dumping).

All this was familiar ground in local authority public relations. What the councils sought by consulting Parliamentary Monitoring Services (PMS) in April 1986 was an assessment of how effective such local measures would be in Parliament, together with recommendations on increasing their impact. The campaign was much assisted early on by the Chernobyl disaster.

Following discussion, it was agreed that councils in the four areas selected for disposal site exploration should form a close-knit coalition to project their views nationally and internationally. This did not need to inhibit local action and protest but would be more effective in gaining media attention and political recognition. Although Essex decided to remain apart, the County Councils Coalition (CCC) was formed and a leaflet produced to set out its views.

It was recognized that protests from MPs in areas selected would achieve only limited response in Parliament. The bulk of members would be quietly relieved that the problem was being tackled outside their own constituencies, and not keen for any change which might alter this scene. Thus a government majority for necessary planning consents was assured. To be properly effective politically the Coalition needed to exploit wider

91

disquiet about radioactive waste disposal in Britain, drawing upon a recent Select Committee for the Environment Report which moved more towards other methods, used elsewhere in Europe. The debate on planning consents should, if possible, be linked to discussion of the Select Committee Report, giving the whole issue a wider, national significance.

While every means of protest should be used at Westminster – with each step publicised as much as possible nationally and locally to sustain momentum – the most effective means of prevention was felt to be through EEC controls. Since Chernobyl there has been a sharpening of views on nuclear and environmental issues in the Community.

All these courses of action were pursued. The CCC proved a working success, particularly in exchange of specialist information and undertaking major CCC initiatives. Literature produced and strength of story at media briefings were more effective as a result.

Always Follow Through

The CCC and its professional advisers were extremely successful in achieving Parliamentary and media attention. In May 1986 they were successful, through lobbying of selected MPs, in achieving a debate in the Commons which linked planning permission with appropriate parts of the Environment Select Committee Report. A media briefing was held on the morning of the Commons debate, television, radio and substantial press resulting. There was also feedback locally through people attending from the Coalition. Lincolnshire's Chief Executive was invited to review the press on BBC Breakfast TV the following day. Although the government achieved its anticipated majority to proceed, a protest was lodged in the House of Lords (using an unfamiliar Parliamentary procedure) which again provided further Parliamentary debate and news coverage.

Large petitions were also delivered by the Coalition councils, each gaining strong local (and some national) attention. Humberside brought its 160,000 signatures to Westminster inside a mock nuclear flask to ensure news pictures. There were of course full briefings for MPs and peers ahead of both debates, ensuring that the CCC points were raised.

A major tenet of the CCC's argument against the NIREX proposals was the comparison with disposal methods under-taken elsewhere in Europe. A delegation from the CCC embarked on a tour of Sweden, West Germany and France to inspect their waste repositories in October 1986. The CCC returned home particularly impressed by the deep-level establish-ments in Forsmark in Sweden and Konrad in West Germany.

A report of the tour and the CCC's second position statement on radioactive waste policy in this country were published at a seminar in London in January 1987. Members of the CCC, local pressure groups, MPs and peers attended. Again widespread media coverage was achieved and questions were asked in the Commons the same afternoon. The CCC was also given the opportunity to debate the issue with members of NIREX on the BBC *Day to Day* programme, screened on the morning of the seminar.

Further Parliamentary debate was secured via a Private Member's Motion soon after the seminar. With the assistance of Michael Brown, Conservative MP for Brigg and Cleethorpes, in whose constituency the Killingholme site is situated, the CCC European Report was fully debated. PMS and the CCC again briefed MPs ahead of the debate and further media coverage was gained. The issue of radioactive waste disposal was also raised during the debate on Sizewell B at the end of February 1987.

The European aspect of the campaign was subsequently pursued on a number of fronts, not simply through UK MEPs but also through members from other countries. This wider dimen-sion is important but often neglected.

The European Parliament's Environment and Energy Com-mittees have been selected as the main instruments for action. A motion calling for the withdrawal of the shallow trench method of disposal, and for the Commission to undertake investigations into alternative methods, was taken up by the Environment Committee. The real pressure, however, lay in close liaison with

European Commissioner Stanley Clinton Davis, who is responsible for the Environment and Nuclear Safety.

The plans also envisaged a CCC delegation to Brussels to discuss radioactive waste disposal with Mr Clinton Davis, his officials from Directorate-Generale XI and MEPs from the Environment and Energy Committees, all of whom were sent the CCC European Tour report. This would give the CCC a further opportunity to maintain the political pressure on the UK Government and NIREX and to gain another news peg.

It worked. At the beginning of May the government announced that it was abandoning the plans to use the four sites – a move naturally attracting Opposition claims that it was a ploy to save votes in the general election, which was held the next month.

Commitment Vital

The importance of total commitment to a cause, the forging of mutually valuable alliances, and detailed monitoring at every stage of the passage of a bill were all graphically highlighted in an excellent booklet published by the Local Government Information Unit, *Lifting the Lid on Lobbying*. In its 29 pages this booklet gives good guidance on 'how legislation is made and how to change it'. One example of its way round the maze dealt with the Social Security Act 1986, published as a Bill at the beginning of that year. Its appearance had been trailered by a green paper and a white paper, and opposition to its proposals was already recorded. In addition, it was a long and complicated piece of legislation.

Within 2 weeks of its publication a local authority team representing the Association of Metropolitan Authorities, the Association of County Councils, and the Local Government Information Unit had been set up. Other opposition was mounted by the trade union movement and by the Child Poverty Action Group.

The main groups set up sub-groups whose task was to plan tactics, handle briefings, and produce amendments to the bill. By means of co-ordinators who managed the sub-groups, this method ensured that all major issues were monitored and dealt with effectively. There was extensive use of both personal and written briefings for MPs of all parties.

One obvious tactic was attendance at Committee sessions. But as the booklet notes:

A relationship with the members was important as note passing by "strangers" is not allowed. It was therefore necessary to catch the eye to get a member to step outside into the corridor if only to accept a note to pass to the front bench.

Obviously the same people could not have been present all the time, as apart from anything else they would have died of boredom. So a co-ordinated shift system was developed so that all sessions were covered. This attendance was important not only to help MPs directly but also for the lobbyists to keep in touch with what was going on – debates, votes, rows, gossip and intelligence.

As demonstrated in other studies, publicity was important 'to raise the profile of the Bill while it was laboriously and often boringly progressing through Committee'. Some opportunities arose during the course of debate but at other times events had to be 'created'. Throughout the proceedings information was fed back to local campaign supporters, and finally, at the end of the Committee, the whole debate was combed 'to identify government evasions, commitments and promises'. That led to further contact, mostly by mail, with both ministers and backbenchers.

The report and third reading were under guillotine, but it was felt that the debate should be on as high and informed a level as possible – and was made so by the work done in Committee. Again, the booklet reminds:

... the Report stage is very important for setting the agenda for the Lords and influencing the outcome of their consideration. A good debate is critical, as is government back bench MPs speaking against their own Ministers. Where a Bill is guillotined it is important to try and ensure that a vote is taken on the key issues, in order to give the right signals to the Lords.

When the bill went to the Lords it created a new situation, described by the Local Government Information Unit thus:

> Peers would be interested in the issues rather than political knockabout, which characterises debates in the Commons. Detailed briefs were necessary. Secondly, they would be impressed by breadth of support for issues, and thirdly they would not want to be lobbied from too many sources. It was therefore decided to formalise the coalition of lobbying groups and create the Social Security Consortium.
>
> The Consortium produced a single briefing on seven issues only, supported by more than 20 organisations – local authorities, trade unions and the voluntary sector. The briefing was bound and was simply produced and each section conformed to a common format – concise, clear and logical. It went to over 200 peers at their home addresses. It was much in evidence in the chamber during Second Reading. At the same time more detailed oral briefings took place with smaller groups of peers.

During the Lords' committee stage careful choice of peers who would agree to move amendments was made. Publicity in the media was brought into play again. In addition:

> Fortunately, the Consortium had access to the skills of a Parliamentary officer of one of its member organisations who had recently worked on the Local Government Bill, and who painstakingly telephoned the Labour peers. Although the government could have mustered its own vote, it was apparently taken by surprise. It had underestimated the peers' traditional concern for children, those with disabilities and for natural justice – and the lobbyists' organisational skills!

The Lords' report stage was different – the government was not going to be caught out again, and won the vote. At the end of it all the bill received the Royal Assent, with some amendments from the original, gained either during the committee stages, the Commons' consideration of the Lords' votes, and the final return to the Lords.

Not all campaigns, however well organized, are successful. Any government with a solid working majority will get its way. But, as made clear elsewhere, campaigns may go on for year after year, chipping away at legislation. Patience is not only a virtue, it is a necessity.

Battling for Birkbeck

On 29 May 1986 an ordinary looking envelope dropped through the letter box at Birkbeck College, London. But its contents were to pose an extraordinary threat to the future of the only university college devoted to face-to-face teaching for part-time degrees.

The letter set out a new formula for calculating Birkbeck's income by the central university funding body, the University Grants Committee (UGC). All Birkbeck students would count only as 0.5 of a full-time student for funding purposes compared with the previous 0.8 of a full-time undergraduate student, with a Birkbeck postgraduate as a full-time equivalent. If this new formula was to be implemented, Birkbeck would lose £2 million, or 30 per cent of its income.

A college campaign committee made up of several professors, the Chairman of the Governors, the Registrar and the President of the Students Union was hastily convened and soon decided to bring in outside help. Enter Charles Barker Watney & Powell, the first major government relations consultancy to work for a university institution. The campaign aimed to put pressure on the UGC and the Department of Education and Science – both publicly and privately through the media and both Houses of Parliament – to review the college's funding formula.

The campaign organizers devised a public relations strategy to highlight the strengths of the Birkbeck system of part-time education and the paradox of the UGC's decision, particularly since the DES had recently published a white paper reiterating its commitment to expanding further education and the role of part-time students. Birkbeck students work by day and study by night. Unlike full-time students, they pay their own fees and pay tax on their earnings. In economic terms they are the most cost-effective students in the UK, and in moral terms they are unconscious bearers of the self-help philosophy embodied in modern Conservatism.

The first step was to ensure that the college was speaking with one voice. So briefing notes, which set out the Birkbeck case, were distributed to all students, former students, staff and governors. They were also sent with a covering letter to an extensive media list, which included education correspondents on the national press, radio and television.

A Special Case

The briefing notes provoked a series of news articles and features which were to make the campaign a national *cause célèbre*. Individual interviews were organized with the Radio 4 *Today* programme and Independent Television News. Opportunities such as a Radio 4 *Tuesday Call* were seized. The college's two main spokesmen and committee chairmen, Professor Roderick Floud and Professor Peter Herriott, both gave numerous media interviews. A series of press statements, marking each stage in the campaign, was issued.

A leader in *The Times* on 27 June 1986 added its weight to the Birkbeck case. Headed 'A Special Case', it concluded:

Mr Kenneth Baker should not shirk from telling the UGC plainly that financial rationalisation must on this occasion be subordinated to the need to encourage – or at least not to discourage – higher education for mature students. Birkbeck is a special case. If necessary, let it be treated as one.

Alongside the press relations campaign, which focused on the educational issues, an effective ground swell of student support was developing into a sustained campaign. T-shirts, lapel badges, and car stickers featuring the slogan 'Join the Battle for Birkbeck' were prepared by Charles Barker and sold through the Student Union shop. A petition with 15,000 student and supporter names, collected in just 2 weeks, was presented to the House of Commons by Dr Keith Hampson MP after a well publicized presentation outside the House of Commons attended by at least a dozen peers and MPs, and one former Secretary of State for Education.

Students, staff, former students and governors were encouraged to write to local MPs and newspapers. Well known former pupils, such as Lord Scarman; supporters, such as Shirley Williams; and Birkbeck academics Ben Pimlott and Roger Scruton placed articles in the national press.

On the Parliamentary front an all-party group of supporters from both Houses was formed. Members included former students, such as Ivor Stanbrook MP and Baroness Jeger, and key supporters, among them Lord Grimond, Lord Fletcher, Dr Keith Hampson MP, Clement Freud (then an MP), Frank Dobson MP, Robert Rhodes James MP and Eric Deakins MP. Many wrote letters on behalf of the college to George Walden, then Under-Secretary of State for Higher Education, and to Kenneth Baker, the Education Secretary. There were two very useful short debates in the House of Lords, when a variety of well known peers and peeresses voiced their concern for the future of the college and praised its academic record. Other MPs tabled questions in the House of Commons.

During the summer an Early Day Motion was tabled in the House of Commons welcoming the increase in numbers of part-time students, urging the government to bring to the attention of the UGC the disastrous consequences of rating part-time students as 0.5 of full-time students, and further urging it to ensure 'a viable future for the only specialist university college in this country dedicated to face-to-face further adult evening education'. By the end of the session this motion, sponsored by Conservative, Labour and one SDP MP, had been signed by fifty-three members. The political pressure was kept up right up until the end of term, with an adjournment debate on Birkbeck College sponsored by Ivor Stanbrook on 25 July just before the start of the summer recess. In replying to the debate the minister said that the prime responsibility lay with the UGC rather than with the government but he hoped that the UGC would take note of the representations that were being made in the House. He ended by saying:

> ... there seems to be no basis at all for the horror stories in the press about the possible closure of Birkbeck College. It is by no means the Government's wish that that should happen – quite the contrary. Our hope is that the good work done by Birkbeck will continue and that the College will continue to offer what are necessary opportunities for part-time study.

The propaganda battle had been won; the government was on the retreat.

In November 1986, at a UGC meeting, Birkbeck's case was reviewed and as a result of a new weighting given to research students a futher £600,000 top-up grant for 1987–8 was awarded to the college. This was a promising start but the basic problem of the future funding arrangements was unaltered. The campaign continued and on 21 November 1986 the Prime Minister herself went on the record: 'We aim to increase still further the proportion of the population which enters our universities, polytechnics and other colleges. I have no doubt that Birkbeck College will continue to make a distinctive and important contribution.'

With the acknowledgement of Birkbeck's key role in higher education came the news from the UGC that the college was to receive 'special factor status'. In the financial years 1987–8 and 1988–9 the new formula would not operate. This reprieve was an interim measure pending the outcome of various enquiries going on within the DES on student funding and within the University of London on sharing the resources of some of the colleges.

This provided time for Birkbeck to regroup for the stage ahead. By then Baroness Tessa Blackstone had been appointed the new Master of Birkbeck College and would add her influential voice to the campaign. A college committee chaired by Sir Barney Hayhoe MP initiated a report on the future structure and financing of the college. It proposed many radical changes to make the college more cost-effective and a major centre for adult education.

In the meantime the allocation of funds from the University of London was still unsatisfactory, as the next Early Day Motion in the House of Commons testified. It read:

That this House regrets the cut in grants to Birkbeck College from the University of London by 6.9 per cent in 1987–88 and provisional projections for subsequent years which show that the level of funding is expected to decline still further to an annual grant of £6.7 million; and calls on Her Majesty's Government to encourage the University of London to provide enough funds to enable the college to continue with its noble tradition of providing face-to-face evening teaching for part-time students on degree courses.

What was achieved was the immediate outburst of protest at Westminster at each suggestion of a cut-back threatening the future of the institution. The ministers at the DES, the UGC and the Court of the University of London were finding it increasingly hard to pass the buck on to one another.

These few studies highlight the importance of the two Ps – planning and persistence. Would-be lobbyists should take them to heart.

8

PARLIAMENT
AT WORK

The Houses of Parliament work within a strict framework of
rules not really as mysterious as many think. In these days of
apparent openness and a freer, more informal approach to the
conduct of public affairs it may seem anachronistic that members
of the House of Commons have to refer to each other in the
Chamber as 'the Member for X' or 'My friend the Right
Honourable etc.' It could be considered more in keeping with the
twentieth century for them to name each other, or to admit that
'my friend' is anything but. This does not seem terribly important, and it is a matter for the House to decide for itself anyway. It
hardly affects the person aiming to influence Parliamentary or
legislative thinking. The rules are bedded deep in the history and
traditions of the House, and are no more surprising or cumbersome than the rules of any professional body or trade union
branch.

They may also have the benefit of occasionally cooling down
tempers to allow reason to overcome prejudice. To the occasional listener to radio broadcasts it may seem surprising that there
are actually rules of debate and procedure, given the bear-garden
atmosphere that seems to prevail, especially at Question Time. In
these circumstances the ability to speak louder than your
opponent or to think up acceptable insults at high speed may
appear greater qualifications than the ability to present a
reasoned case or a set of facts. It may be equally puzzling to
understand how such proceedings really help in the governing of

the country. The fact is that this knockabout stuff bears about as much relation to the serious business of the House as one-day cricket does to the proper game.

First comes the order of business. Some of the items are only taken after due notice has been posted, and are starred below. The others do not need notice, and may thus not appear on the order paper but will be taken at the appropriate time if they come up. Notification of the Royal Assent to Acts can be given at any time through the day, with the business interrupted accordingly.

Business always starts with prayers. These are followed by the Queen's answers to Addresses, formal notices from the Speaker, motions for new writs, private business (*), presentation of public petitions, and motions for unopposed returns (*).

Next comes question time (*) – oral answer first, followed by private notice questions. After questions come ministerial statements, the introduction of new members, proposals to move the adjournment (Mondays to Thursdays only), motions for leave of absence, ceremonial speeches, giving notice of motions and holding a ballot (*), personal explanations, the consideration of amendments from the Lords (if they are brief and easily dealt with), and matters of privilege.

Notice will have been given for most of the rest of the day's business, which comprises the presentation of public, i.e. government, bills, government motions, motions for leave to bring in bills or nominate select committees, and the orders of the day and notice of motions as in the daily order paper, all taken in the order in which they are printed. The order paper gives notice of the day's proceedings, lists all the questions due to come up, both for oral and written answer, as well as giving the list of committees sitting that day.

Place of questions

For many people of course, including journalists, questions provide entertainment coupled with information. Part of a minister's skill may lie in observing the well practised political art of not answering the question asked but what he would have liked the question to ask (or not ask, as the case may be). With those down for oral answer this tactic may lead him into a minefield of supplementaries, which the Speaker can terminate if he feels a subject has been well enough aired. Questions are asked for various reasons – to elicit information, to irritate or embarrass a government, to air a view, or to permit a minister to say something or make an announcement for which there is no other clear early opportunity.

Give or take a minute or two, questions last just under one hour. They must be handed in with two days' clear notice (except on Mondays and Tuesdays, when they can be handed in by 2.30 for answer the following Wednesday and Thursday). They cannot be submitted more than 10 days ahead of the date for answer. Ministers have set days for answering questions addressed to their department, with the Prime Minister taking hers on Tuesdays and Thursdays, for 15 minutes each time. The order in which departmental questions are answered is decided after all those put down have been tossed into a hat and drawn (metaphorically), so that the principle of fair shares for all shall apply. No Member can have more than two questions down for any one day, but, subject to the discretion of the Speaker, can ask supplementaries.

The time allotted dictates the number of questions actually given oral answers, but the official report of the day's business (*Hansard* published next morning) gives answers to every question printed in the order paper. Members may also submit questions for which they are happy to accept a written answer. There is no limit to these and they are included in the official report.

There is place in the timetable for private notice questions only if the Speaker deems the matter to be of genuine and urgent public interest. Such a matter could be a natural disaster like an earthquake needing instant relief action, and thus a statement of intent or support from the government. Private notice questions cannot be asked if what they raise already appears in some form in a previously tabled question.

The press of questions – something like 30,000 a year – is such that they can only be part of the armoury of a lobby or pressure group. There have been members in the past – there are probably today, and there will be tomorrow – who ask questions because it gets their name in the media, especially in their local paper. There are those who are specialists in a particular subject and who look for opportunities to ventilate it. In general, however, questions are asked because information that apparently cannot be obtained any other way is sought. Often enough, if a member is asked by a constituent, local organization, or pressure group to find some information, he can get it fairly easily from the appropriate Ministry direct or by writing to the minister.

Types of Bills

It has to be said that questions are one of the few ways in which a backbench MP can fulfil the late Andy Warhol's comment that everybody is famous for a few minutes. They are seldom occasions when a minister can be sufficiently outwitted to reveal something he would have preferred to keep hidden. Since questions are tabled in advance, the minister has time to get his answer together and to anticipate most of the supplementaries.

The House will then get down to the consideration of bills. There are three kinds: public bills, private members' bills and private bills.

Public Bills are presented by the government. Normally the intention to present them will have been signalled in general tems in the manifesto published before a general election, and further explained in either a green paper or white paper (or even a white paper with green edges). Notice that they are to be introduced in the next session (which runs from November to October) comes in the Queen's Speech. The theory is that supporters and opponents have good advance warning and can prepare their case. It does not always happen. Governments sometimes bring in bills without any notice and sometimes fail to get round to bills they intended to get through.

In certain circumstances, usually not very admirable, a bill can be rushed through at great speed, especially if the government can be sure of a majority big enough to allow even some of the members of its own party to abstain or vote against. Usually, however, bills do take several months to become Acts.

The stages are carefully set down. The bill is formally introduced at its first reading, when there is no debate. A date is set for the second reading, and the bill is then printed and made available from the Stationery Office.

Debate at the second reading is largely concerned with the principles of the bill, and will cover a good deal of ground for the day it will normally last. The debate allows the government further to test reactions, possibly to hear from specialists in the subject on both sides of the House and to have flaws exposed.

Then comes the real work, as the bill moves into the committee stage. The committee – 17–50 members in number – is balanced to reflect the size of the parties in the House, and goes through the bill clause by clause. Committees are open to the public, who would mostly be people with a direct interest. Meetings are held in the mornings, twice a week, and continue for several weeks. Outside the meetings members will consult special interest groups or experts. The examination of a bill is an exhaustive process, and its progress may well be dictated by the chairman, who will be a senior member of the House.

The Lords Move In

At the conclusion of the examination the amended bill goes back to the House for the report stage, when it is further amended or new clauses are added. The report stage can also be lengthy, though in terms of days not weeks. It is followed immediately by the formal third reading, by which the House announces its agreement that the bill can go to the Lords. In the Upper House the same stages are taken, except that the committee stage takes place in the Chamber and takes less time (debate on the floor of the Commons for the committee stage of a bill usually only applies to constitutional issues).

There is then the opportunity for a little ping-pong. The Lords returns the bill with its suggested amendments. The Commons either accepts them or rejects them. If it rejects them, the bill returns to the Lords for a second time, with the Commons' reasons for the rejection, and the House of Lords has another think. If it fails to agree, the House of Commons has the final say, which may take up to a year. This amendment to procedure was introduced by the Labour Government of 1949 to prevent the Lords, as an unelected body, being able to control legislation.

The bill then receives the Royal Assent (the last time the Sovereign refused was in 1707) and becomes law that day, unless there has been some special provision for it to become law at another time. Some Acts require orders to bring them into force.

Public bills do not normally fail. If the government has a sufficient working majority and has laid its ground efficiently, almost any measure it wants can be taken through, even if it has to be forced through by the use of the guillotine, which lays down a timetable. That does not mean that even major amendments cannot be achieved. With time and equally careful planning, the efficient pressure group can sometimes work wonders.

Private members' bills succeed less frequently. To have any chance they must be near the top of the ballot or have the sympathetic support of the government. The procedure starts on the second Thursday of a session, when the names of twenty members are drawn and they are given first call on whatever Parliamentary time the government is prepared to allow to private members. Since the government controls the timetable and may well want to monopolize most of it for its own business, private members do not get very much time, – actually only 13 days in a session. When names come out, the members concerned may have a subject ready. In any event the top twenty are quickly buttonholed by outside interests who hope they can persuade the lucky ones to introduce a bill on their chosen interest. The jockeying will go on for another 3 weeks, at the end of which the Members have to state what bill they are going to submit.

Some of them are obviously put forward just to air a subject that has no hope of obtaining legislative backing but on which the discussion alone may prompt government action at some later stage. Some are so clearly non-contentious or at the least

107

able to command all-party support that they can be considered likely runners. If the government is openly antagonistic, the bill stands no chance – a point often made to aspiring sponsors by the pressure group that is looking for an opening.

Backbench members face a further difficulty. Acts of Parliament are the law of the land, and have to be drafted by solicitors (in this context, Parliamentary agents), with their convoluted use of language. Governments can call on a battery of drafters and even then produce bills whose effects are sometimes not at all what was intended. A badly drawn up private bill can be easily demolished by opposition. Eric Taylor, author of one of the early books about Parliament (*The House of Commons at Work*) emphasized the point:

> . . . to draft a document so that it will convey exactly the meaning it is intended to convey and not, by any stretch of interpretation, another meaning, even under the pressure of law court proceedings – so that it will say what has to be said adequately and clearly, and not say anything it is not meant to say – is a highly skilled task . . . every new Act that is passed in a highly developed society such as ours, is bound to interfere with someone's happiness and peace of mind, and to trench upon established interests somewhere.

Members who introduce bills have to be single-minded and extremely determined to have any hope of success.

Other Procedures

Once published, private members' bills go through the same procedure as public ones, but the amount of time allowed for them to be debated, in committee as well as in the Chamber, is strictly limited. The wonder sometimes is that any of them get through.

Backbench MPs have a further opportunity in the Ten Minute Rule, so called because speeches for and against a motion are limited to that time. At the start of public business on Tuesdays and Wednesdays a member may ask for leave of the House to introduce a bill. He is then allowed to explain – in 10 minutes – and an opponent is allowed equal time. The House is then asked either to throw out the bill or allow it to proceed through the usual stages. Most times it is sudden death, but the method has the great advantage of allowing a member to speak on a matter he or his allies consider important enough to merit the attention of the House at a time when it is often fairly full, i.e. just after questions.

The proportion of private members' bills that become law is small – the 1984–5 session was unusual in that 21 reached the statute book, while 97 were unsuccessful. At random the figures for some other years were 13 successful and 105 unsuccessful in 1983–4 (admittedly a long session); 10 successful and 115 unsuccessful in 1979–80; and 11 successes against 78 failures in 1976–7 and again in 1977–8.

There remains the private bill, introduced and intended to benefit 'a person or a body of persons'. Most of them come from local authorities, public bodies or organizations like water boards. They are originated by petition, and may start in either House. The committee stage is different in that the appointed committee examines witnesses and hears counsel in public sessions. Opposition usually comes from individuals or organizations who feel they will be directly harmed if the bill becomes an Act. A degree of vigilance is called for to spot them happening, though public announcements are made well ahead, often in local papers.

Individuals or organizations who feel their interests threatened by a private bill can express their opposition by means of a petition, on which a strict timetable applies. The Private Bill Office in the House of Commons advises on the rules to be observed. One aspect of private bills merits attention. Such a bill can be presented by a private group seeking authority to provide a public service. In an atmosphere in which privatization is being considerably encouraged it is not unlikely that such authority will be sought more frequently (however relative 'frequently' is). Those who will be affected need to keep a watchful eye.

A final opportunity to raise a particular subject is the Adjournment Debate, usually for half an hour every day at the end of public business. Subjects are submitted by backbench members and a ballot is held for the right to initiate the debate. In the last days before a recess (i.e. 2 or 3 weeks at Christmas, one at Easter and the Spring Bank Holiday, and just under 3 months from August to early October) the motion is moved that the House should take a break for the agreed period and there follows a 3-hour debate. In practice members can raise any subject they like in this time.

The Adjournment

The adjournment debate is popular because it allows a backbencher to speak at some length on a subject dear to his heart or dear to the pressure group he supports. It gets a government response from a junior minister, who will also wish to show his prowess, especially if the matter under discussion is controversial. However, it suffers from its timing. It is seldom reached before late at night, when the attendance is usually sparse and when the press and television have virtually closed for the night. It is thus extremely unlikely to get much public attention. It may have a value in 'testing the water' and is not to be ignored, but it needs to be seen in perspective as a way of achieving any real effect.

On a few occasions the House will agree to an adjournment debate on a 'matter of urgent public consideration'. This is raised by a member at the start of public business and, provided the Speaker and the House agree, is debated either early that evening or at the same time the following day. The idea is tried out many times in each session but in practice usually fails to secure the support of the necessary quorum.

Members can also put down an Early Day Motion. It will not be debated at the time, and may just give a member the opportunity to find out whether the subject of the motion has enough sympathy from the House for him to try to take it further.

In 1978 an attempt to reassert Parliament's power over events was proposed by the Select Committee on Procedure. It was a personal triumph for Norman St John Stevas, who, as the editor of Bagehot's classic *The English Constitution*, was a great believer in the rights and duties of Parliament. The proposal was to establish new 'watchdog' committees, to be composed of backbench MPs and each given authority to keep an eye on individual Departments of State. Fourteen were set up. The chairman of each was a senior member who had not had any relation with the department with which his committee was concerned – for instance, a minister in a former government would not have been picked. The committees cover agriculture, defence, education, science and the arts, employment, energy, the environment, foreign affairs, home affairs, industry and trade, Scottish affairs, Welsh affairs, social services and transport, and the Treasury and Civil Service. There is also a public accounts committee; and EEC draft proposals are examined by the European legislation committee, which decides whether they should be debated by the full House.

The select committees have power to call expert witnesses and to question civil servants, and are always very ready to hear from interested groups or individuals, especially if they have genuine expertise in the subject. The public accounts committee deals with money spent rather than money to be spent in the future, and tends to concern itself mostly with good housekeeping. Unlike the others, the chairman is usually someone with ministerial experience in a financial department and is always an opposition MP.

There is a fair turnover of members, and some noticeable differences in the way the committees operate. Some are necessarily somewhat secretive, such as the Foreign Affairs committee, while others are as open to Commons' hurly-burly as the floor of the House itself. Supporters of the system maintain that the committees have brought back some of the backbencher's traditional belief in his influence, a point of some debate.

Governments do not like the committees because they can be inquisitive about matters they might prefer not to discuss. A degree of deliberate frustrating by government is sometimes

111

evident. Discussion in committees tends to be less frenetic than in the Chamber. Few senior members – present ministers and former ministers in other governments – have ever been members of a select committee, but as the system goes on this must change. A committee can be a way for an ambitious younger member (younger in service in the House, whether younger in age or not) to make himself known, though he may have to pick his committee and his words with some care. The names of members are easily available.

Parliamentary Groups

A much older system is that of the single-party groups and the all-party ones. All parties have groups of backbenchers who are expert in a subject, or just interested in it. They are formed partly to be present at and speak in debates on the subject and to keep a watching brief on the doings of relevant departments, and partly to keep their own senior members – ministers or shadow ministers – informed of party opinion from the lowest levels upwards. Parties pick the chairman, vice-chairman and secretary, and any backbench MP is free to join. Parties also have groups of regional members – Welsh, West Midland, Greater London are examples – which are also ways for party leaders to keep in touch, try out ideas, and rally support. Lists of the members are available from party head offices.

Dating back originally to the thirties are the all-party groups. They were formed to help backbenchers keep up-to-date on given subjects and, as their name makes clear, cross party boundaries. At the present there are almost 100. Some are permanent, like the Parliamentary and Scientific Committee, which goes back to 1939, but others can be short-lived. Some are directly concerned with industrial matters. The list can be had from the Commons Public Information Office. The all-party groups are an enduring and vitally useful institution, providing government with a sounding board, members with facts, and pressure groups with an opening. Outsiders may and do attend meetings, but there are now strict rules about the groups' composition, their funding, and their ability to meet in rooms in the Palace of Westminster.

Some members make a fetish of seeing robbers under the bed in the way that these committees (and other Commons bodies) are financially supported or open to sectional interests. The use of the House for lunches, sponsored exhibitions or presentations, and the direct links between committees or individual members and pressure groups are meat and drink to members who are adept or wish to be at showing up the other side. Nevertheless it must be said that the occasional exposure of actual mis-deeds or attempts to suborn the House is no bad thing in a democracy.

Lastly come the Scottish and Welsh Grand Committees. To them are referred bills which deal exclusively with the interests of the two countries. As with all committees, membership reflects the balance of power in the House.

The House of Lords operates to many of the same basic rules as the Commons, but for the seeker of influence it is important to remember that the value of the Upper House lies more in the expression of wisdom, expertise and more or less impartial judgement than in real power. Bills from the government of the day go through the same procedures, except that they tend to move more quickly and that the Committee stage is taken on the floor, i.e. a committee of the whole House. The Lords can propose amendments, bring to bear on the discussion a fund of knowledge, and see consequences that may have escaped the Commons – but in the end that House cannot prevent a Bill becoming law. It can only delay it.

During the life of a Parliament the government will use the Lords as the jumping-off point of some bills, usually if they are non-contentious. European documents go to the Lords and are studied in detail by one of seven committees, which can call for witnesses and other experts. Broadly speaking the Lords has more time than the Commons, and its members are less concerned with personal publicity. It is generally recognized that the quality of debate is somewhat higher and more dignified than in the Commons, and it is certainly less susceptible to the slanging matches that regularly disfigure the good name of Parliament.

Getting Information

Information in detail about the House and its doings is readily available. The 'Bundle' for the Commons and 'Minutes of Proceedings' for the Lords appear every day that Parliament sits, and can be bought. All bills and other papers can be obtained from that storehouse of information, the Stationery Office. Prestel provides daily summaries, and a subscription to POLIS (Parliamentary On-line Information System) can be taken out.

The best starting point for those unfamiliar with Parliament is probably the public information offices for both Houses, and their helpful staff. Select-committee work is published in *The Daily Telegraph*, or can be had from the committees' own permanent staffs. House of Lords committees' details are published weekly, or an approach may be made to the Clerk of the Committee.

The general switchboard of the House will either put a caller straight through to the right person, or will give the correct direct number.

When all is finished and done with, Parliament is where legislation comes from. Wherever and however it starts, it ends at Westminster. Some of the rules of procedure and debate could probably be dispensed with, and the House does not seem to have woken up entirely to twentieth-century technology. But it would be a brave person who would radically alter it, or even tinker with it. Democracy is a fragile enough flower and if 'my right honourable friend' has to be called that, even when he is a notorious rogue, it is immaterial. There are times when the end really does justify the means.

9

OUR DECISION –
OR THEIRS?

A riddle wrapped in a mystery inside an enigma was how Winston Churchill once described the USSR. For most people in Britain today he could well have been talking about the European Commission and the European Parliament. Yet it is vital for business people to understand both before 1992.

There is a running debate in the British Parliament about the dangers of losing our sovereignty, with decisions taken in Brussels or Strasbourg now affecting the conduct of our affairs, superseding and changing our own domestic laws. This has seemed to surprise many people, despite the fact that when we joined in 1972, we knew that part of Jean Monnet's conception of a federated states of Europe meant sharing a measure of sovereignty. The idea that permanent peace could replace recurring war was pleasing, but few appear to have understood that it meant adopting common policies if it could be argued that they offered a prospect of greater universal benefit. These policies were and are in general economic. The British view of Europe, as expressed in the media and in many speeches, tends to be clouded by the apparently unfathomable mysteries of some of the proposals on harmonization, coupled with the traditional British suspicion of those strange people across the Channel.

A typical recent example is the knotty question of product liability, under which a manufacturer and/or his suppliers can be held responsible for defects in his products. The scope of the European directive on this subject is enormously wide, but we cannot avoid it in this country. We have agreed to change our own laws within 3 years from the passing of the European rules in 1986.

Progress to the European idea and ideal has been bedevilled and slowed down by two things. One is the Common Agricultural Policy, in which the only common link has probably been each government's watchful eye on the all-important farmers' vote. The other is a variation on the same theme: the need for each government to consider the effect of a 'European' decision on its own national interests. As the Community has grown in numbers, this factor has contributed even more to the snail's pace at which things often appear to happen.

To the outsider the EEC seems to have done little more than spawn a vast bureaucracy in Brussels, with more than 10,000 civil servants squabbling in the nine official languages, earning enormous tax-free salaries, daily destroying countless acres of trees to produce reams of paper for documents that few ever read, really achieving little, and generally leading the life of Riley. Further south, the European Parliament in Strasbourg is considered a monstrous irrelevancy.

Like it or not, the Community is a fact. It cannot be pushed to one side and asked – politely even – to go away. Although in its workings it is fairly byzantine, its ways have to be unravelled and understood. The alternative is to abdicate responsibility for the political decisions that make our lives what they are. That attitude is totally indefensible. It is also pie in the sky to claim that we could negotiate our way out of the EEC.

EEC Structure

Among other objectives the Community exists (or is supposed to exist) to work towards the improvement of the ordinary citizen's living and working conditions; agreed common action to 'guarantee' steady expansion, balanced trade and fair competition; and the progressive abolition of restrictions on international trade. It is in three parts – the European Coal and Steel Community, the European Atomic Energy Community, and the

European Economic Community (popularly known as the Common Market). We are mostly concerned with the last.

It is controlled and administered by the Parliament, the Council of Ministers, the Commission, the Court of Justice, and the Court of Auditors.

Parliament has the duty to maintain democratic control over the Community, with its members elected every 5 years.

The Council of Ministers has twelve members. It meets three times a year, and meetings are attended by ministers specializing in the subject to be discussed, whether it be agriculture, finance or whatever, and for major occasions by foreign ministers. It takes the final decisions on Europe-wide laws.

The Commission is the executive body. There are fourteen commissioners with support staffs. It proposes new laws, or initiatives, monitors how each member country is observing the laws, and acts as the administrator of agreed policies.

The Court of Justice is the supreme legal body for judgement of disputes over the application or interpretation of the Community law.

The Court of Auditors checks the management of the finances (however unlikely that sometimes appears!)

The European Parliament is elected on universal suffrage as in Britain. In Britain itself, England provides 66 constituencies, Scotland 8, and Wales 4. Northern Ireland operates as one constituency, providing 3 MEPs (Members of the European Parliament) elected by proportional representation. The constituency boundaries bear little relation to those of the domestic Parliament. MEPs debate major public issues affecting the Community; consider and amend Commission-proposed new laws; and decide the annual budget, in conjunction with the Commission. Members of the Council of Ministers and the Commission attend debates and answer questions. In theory Parliament can dismiss the Commission, though it is difficult to conceive circumstances in which this might happen. Just as in the House of Commons an assiduous MEP can learn how to manipulate the system.

EEC Methods

The business of each session of Parliament is decided by the Bureau, co-operating with the chairmen of the political groups. The Bureau is composed of the President and vice-presidents, who are elected for a term of 2½ years. Periods are set aside for questions to the Council, the Commission and foreign ministers. As well as the consideration of reports from committees, there are general debates on Community policies; and there is a procedure for emergency debates. As in Britain, written questions can be submitted. The other major check the Parliament can exercise is to reject the Commission's budget – which it has done. The budget decision is taken in December, at the end of the financial and calendar year. Delays have more than once meant the whole European idea teetering on the brink of bankruptcy, or appearing to do so.

Most of the detailed work, again as at Westminster, is handled in committee. There are eighteen of them, covering politics, agriculture, budgets, economic and monetary questions, energy and research, external trade, legal affairs, social and employment questions, regional policy and planning, transport, the environment, health and the consumer, youth, culture, education, and sport, overseas development, budgetary control, procedure, members' credentials, institutional affairs, and the situation of women.

The committees examine the Commission's actions, draft laws and go over any other issues deemed worthy of attention. Membership reflects the balance of the political groups – with more than sixty parties represented. They hold public hearings and can call in experts and specialists to give evidence. The Commission is bound to give advance notice of its plans and intentions to Parliament, so that they can be debated.

All this is laborious and obviously leads to delay upon delay. However, that is inevitable in any organization as big and as new as the Community. Its downside – slowness – is nevertheless an opportunity. It does give those hoping to influence the passage of laws, regulations, and directives time in which to work.

The contact with MEPs is made in exactly the same way as with MPs. A list is available any time from the European Parliament Information Office in London. It should be remembered though that a European MP has to be concerned with European issues and be conscious of European attitudes, and is working on a bigger stage than his domestic counterpart.

There is recourse for the individual or organization feeling aggrieved. Contact with an MEP or with the relevant political party is not difficult. The approach can be made to a committee of the Parliament, with the ultimate – probably grand is a better word – gesture of petitioning the Parliament by writing direct to the President.

Some MEPs are members of both Parliaments, but this could justifiably be regarded as an unwelcome development. It is difficult to believe that anybody can pay proper attention to the needs of both assemblies. The House of Commons is busy enough and difficult enough to master without having to learn a whole new series of procedures and ideas, especially in a multi-language environment. Just as a person running or managing a commercial enterprise has to concentrate and avoid as much distraction as possible, so an MP, British or European, has to establish priorities in the use of time. It seems wrong to have to learn to jump over two sets of fences at the same time. The situation only applies to a handful of members but it is to be hoped it does not spread.

The Commission

Dealing with the Commission is different from dealing with the Parliament, and comparable with dealing with the Civil Service. First we must understand its role and organization.

The Commission makes proposals for policy, after its officials have consulted as many interested parties as possible and whatever specialists are available. It also acts as a mediator between the member governments, as does the Civil Service between ministries in Britain.

Finally, it implements policies agreed by the Council of

Ministers. It has been called the conscience of the community. At its core are about 1,000 senior civil servants from the fourteen countries. Even with all their back-up staffs, totalling about 12,000, it is not really the swollen monster it is sometimes portrayed as in the popular press. The organization is fairly straightforward.

The fourteen Commissioners, elected for a 4-year term, choose a president and, at the moment, five vice-presidents, who serve for 2 years but whose terms of office can be renewed. No country can have more than two commissioners. Each takes responsibility for a particular aspect of the Commission's duties. They meet weekly, usually in Brussels, but in Luxembourg or Strasbourg when the Council of Ministers or European Parliament are meeting. There are nineteen directorates-general, covering all the predictable subjects from trade to agriculture, from consumer protection to regional policy.

When the Commission decides to move on a subject, which it may do either on its own initiative or at the behest of the Council of Ministers, it embarks on a programme of extensive consultation. This may be undertaken by civil servants in the Commission or by a specialist consultative or advisory committee, either standing or set up for the purpose. The programme is bound to be lengthy, for obvious reasons.

The Economic and Social Assembly is an important body for the lobbyist. On certain matters it must be consulted by the Commission, but it can also take up matters on its own initiative. It has 156 members, who represent employers, trade unions, and special interest groups. They are nominated by the government of their own country, serve for 4 years, and can be re-elected. It has nine sections, which carry out detailed studies of matters affecting their special interests.

Effect of EEC Law

Laws in the Community take various forms and they are all binding on member states, who have to alter or amend their own laws as necessary. In most cases there is a period of grace

120

between a Community decision and its implementation by a member country. There are four instruments open to the Commission:

1 *Regulations*, which have the full force of law, and must be observed by all countries.
2 *Decisions*, which are also legally binding on the organziation or individual at whom they are directed. This can be a government, an industry in one or several countries, or a professional body.
3 *Directives*, which may be intended for only one country rather than all and whose interpretation and implementation in detail is up to those to whom they have been delivered.
4 *Recommendations*, which are the exception in that they can be ignored.

Any wise company should be equipped to monitor European legislation, particularly regulations and directives. As elsewhere, ignorance is no defence. It is equally wise to be able to suck through the pipeline as much information as possible on broad policy trends, trade flow and opinion shifts.

'Find the official' is the name of the game. The published lists are a good starting point. An invitation to make a visit is acceptable, preferably face-to-face in Brussels. The rules are not dissimilar to those applying in Britain, even if it costs rather more to play by them. In this instance it is also essential to be as well armed with background, statistics, facts and a carefully reasoned case before making the first move. The Commission is not actually awash with bureaucrats – for the population and interests they serve there is a relatively small body of officials and they are generally extremely busy. Like the tax-man they will pay courteous attention, but they will only investigate or act on a case that is well put. Clearly it is marginally more difficult for the individual businessman or company to raise problems or desires in Brussels than in London, so it is sensible to be aware that many professional bodies, trade associations and large companies have permanent offices in Brussels and regular contact with

Berlaymont officials. It may be much more effective to work with them, especially at the beginning.

The importance of what goes on in the EEC can hardly be exaggerated. Complaining about the prospect of diminished sovereignty is pointless. Suggestions that we should withdraw are futile. We are in it and we can change it, as Mrs Thatcher has done more than once. Recognize where it impinges, and even more valuably where it might in the future, and you are on the way to influencing it.

All information is available from the Stationery Office in the EEC official journal or monthly bulletin, the DTI publication *British Business*, the London offices of the Parliament or the Commission's offices in London, Edinburgh, Cardiff and Belfast. In Brussels itself, apart from the obvious sources, much helpful guidance will be given by the personnel in the office of the UK Permanent Representative (UKREP).

10

MALIGN OR
BENEVOLENT?

In 1946 Francis Williams, the distinguished left-inclined journalist, wrote (*Press, Parliament and People*):

Although their (newspapers') long-term influence in serious
affairs is small and their effect on their readers' political
thinking negligible, they often exert a good deal of influence on
Ministers and government departments. Most cabinet ministers are indeed almost excessively sensitive to newspaper
comment. That is all to the good. It is better that Ministers
should trouble themselves too much about newspaper criticism than too little. Anything that keeps great government
departments constantly aware that they are the servants of the
public and are liable to a public reprimand if they do not do
their work properly is an advantage.

Something over 30 years later, James Margach, another distinguished journalist though perhaps more to the right than the left,
wrote (*The Abuse of Power*):

. . . the tempestuous and never-ending war between Downing
Street and Fleet Street, Whitehall and the Press . . . (I) have seen
at first hand the complex and fascinating exercise of real power
in a war which has been neglected to an astonishing extent. To
win this war has been the first priority of nearly all the dozen
Prime Ministers I have known. With almost obsessional

ruthlessness the majority sought to dominate and influence the Press, TV and radio as the vital precondition to their domination of Parliament, parties and public opinion. First to establish and fortify their personal power and second to reinforce the conspiracy of secrecy, to preserve the sanctity of government behind the walls of Whitehall's forbidden city.

Some things do not change. Mrs Thatcher's Press Secretary, Bernard Ingham, maintained a running battle with the press, accusing it of distortion, incorrect emphasis, and many other sins. In one speech covering the current condition of journalism, its ethics and the journalist's role in society, he remarked bitterly of 'a cavalier approach to facts, especially if inconvenient, and a certain amnesia when it comes to checking; a readiness to make deductions which are as creative in their approach to logic as some accounting is to sound finance; and an excess of malice'.

More recently, former Conservative Party chairman Norman Tebbit spied what he saw as the growing influence of television and put the BBC in the dock, claiming that it was riddled with bias against Conservatism and used its programmes to promote left-wing, i.e. subversive, ideas. Harold Wilson, when Prime Minister, was notorious for believing the media was out to get him.

Left – or Right?

It is fairly easy to detect sinister influences at work in the content of television programmes. In one study by the Media Monitoring Unit it was claimed that 150 programmes in a 12-month period were 'left-wing'. The survey was carried out by a man who admitted to being 'right of centre'. While accepting that he must have done his best not to be over-critical or extra-analytical, one is forced to the feeling that if he had been 'left of centre', he might have seen it differently. Most of the time the eye sees what it wants to see and the mind receives signals it is predisposed to receive.

Malign or benevolent? Of course the media is neither all of the time and both some of the time. It is also just as capable of self-deception as any government. It is pleased to be remembered for Burke's remark (which he may not have made) when pointing to the reporters' gallery in the House of Commons: 'Yonder sits the Fourth Estate, more important than them all' (the other three were the Lords Temporal, the Lords Spiritual, and the Commons itself). It does exercise influence. It is now rather different from the heyday of the press super-barons of the thirties, Beaverbrook and Rothermere, but it is very much there. It can and does expose corruption, deceit, and the now popular word, disinformation. That is why it is disliked by politicians.

Francis Williams said: '... the public ought to be able to turn to newspapers for a coherent explanation and criticism of government measures and for a steady and unsullied supply of information on all matters of political and social importance'. As an ideal to be aimed at this can hardly be bettered, but before trying to decide whether it is attainable or not, it is worth seeing how much people care.

Lord Northcliffe, the founding father of modern tabloid journalism, said that the average newspaper reader was not interested in politics. This arbitrary decision, not backed by any research, allowed him and his successors to spawn a whole series of daily papers more concerned with titillation and relative trivialities than with serious issues. A 1963 survey by the International Publishing Corporation on the other hand showed that only one issue had above average readership – home politics. Even if that is true, it is difficult to see any reflection of it in the 'popular' dailies, beyond occasionally hysterical leading articles about mugging, rape, hooliganism, and the despair of the elders at the general behaviour of the younger generation, or vice-versa. It is different at election time, when generous space is devoted to the parties, and papers set out their preferences clearly. One is bound to wonder how the reader can form a sensible view on competing claims when he has not been brought into the arena with sufficient background.

Media Content

In so far as democracy is about the opportunity for freedom of individual choice then the press is a fine example of democracy in action. Britain is unique in the structure of its press in having national daily and Sunday papers which ensure that the same news is seen – allowing for different editions as the news develops through the night – by the reader in Aberdeen or Penzance. Of the current eleven morning papers, one is a specialist (*Financial Times*), four others are 'serious' (*The Times, The Independent, The Guardian, The Daily Telegraph*), one has a tiny circulation (*Morning Star*, the former *Daily Worker*), and the rest are 'popular'. Of the Sundays, three are serious (*The Sunday Times, The Observer* and the *Sunday Telegraph*) and the rest are popular, although the *Sunday Express* would claim to be in the serious category.

On any fairly typical day *The Times* will devote about 10 per cent of its editorial content to political stories; *The Daily Telegraph* about 5 per cent; *The Independent* and *The Guardian* about 8 per cent; and the *Financial Times* about 15 per cent. All give a page at least to reports of the previous day in Parliament, most carry regular political analysis, and some carry a 'sketch' – a personal view of the proceedings by a named writer. As to the analysis, it is worth recording that interpreting, or trying to interpret, political signals is a highly complicated game, but it is only a game. It is played by media commentators, in and out of Parliament, who are usually more anxious to prove their ability as tipsters than to be either right or taken too literally. Thus the forecasts are usually hedged with ifs, buts and maybes. When the fact becomes known, like theatre managers they extract the quote that demonstrates their cleverness. It is likely to be out of context.

Backing the dailies are a number of outstanding regional and Scottish papers – for example, in England and Wales there are the *Birmingham Post, The Journal* in Newcastle, the *Yorkshire Post* in Leeds, the *Western Daily Press* in Bristol, and the *Western Mail* in Cardiff; while in Scotland there are the *Glasgow Herald* and *The Scotsman* in Edinburgh. Most regional dailies are linked to evening papers, which as a rule pay only passing attention to political matters and then tend to concentrate, rightly, on local relevance.

There is clearly no lack of opportunity either to present or to hear different points of view.

A further source is the national weekly papers, where it may be argued that more consistent attention is paid to the political, social and economic issues facing the nation. *The Economist, The Spectator,* the *New Statesman* and *Tribune* all come into this category. Even if their circulations are relatively small, their influence can be great. As has been perceptively pointed out, the Press may not persuade the public directly, but it is the means by which people get to know about things and form their own judgements; and as Francis Williams (and many others since him) well recognized, politicians pay close attention to what is being written.

Press Attitudes

The trade and technical press must not be ignored. Britain is awash with trade and technical periodicals appearing weekly, monthly, quarterly and a few twice a week or twice a year. Many of them are staffed by writers who know their subject inside out. Those where the editor is a journalist rather than a trained and qualified specialist in the trade or profession for which he is writing will use outside contributors to provide the expert reporting, interpretation and comment. Some publish a regular political column, unsigned when written by a moonlighting Parliamentary journalist or specialist freelance, otherwise written (possibly ghosted) by an MP. As with the 'political' weeklies, the influence of these papers may be small in quantity but much higher in quality, though much of the view is retrospective.

It is then necessary to consider what sort of view the press is putting forward, on both the long-standing or suddenly arising questions about our society. It is a constant criticism by the Labour Party, socialist and radical groups that the press is controlled by a small number of proprietors whose inclinations will always be to support a conservative or right-wing government. The standard proprietors' response is that they do not interfere in editorial policy.

Both positions are ultimately suspect. It is obvious that the senior members of the editorial team of any newspaper are likely to be in sympathy with the owner's views but to suggest that they follow them slavishly in their writing borders on insult. It was widely said in Fleet Street that Beaverbrook, the 'free-trade-and-Empire-forever' campaigner, had more Socialists on his staff than any other paper. Indeed he was famous for hiring left-wing writers. What is different today is the circumstances in which newspapers are owned and published. Beaverbrook bought himself into journalism because it gave him a vehicle to promote his political views (he was also a fine journalist). The fact that he largely failed is immaterial. Today's proprietors have to solve a different problem before they can start thinking too clearly about exercising that sort of influence. Newspapers are up against television, a more mobile population and a host of other competing demands on people's time in a way that the owners of 50 years ago never dreamed of. Newspapers have to concentrate on profitability far more than once was the case. It is no accident that most owners have interests well outside daily or Sunday papers. It is therefore a tenable argument, as advanced by James Curran and Jean Seaton (*Power Without Responsibility*) that

> . . . national newspapers emphasise collective values (eg: the national interest) and collective symbols of identification (eg: the monarch) in a way that fosters national rather than class solidarity. Above all, nationals foster the belief that the political and social structure is natural – the way things are – by depicting reality as a series of more or less discrete events.

In order to be profitable, daily papers have two options. They must cut costs or sell more advertising. They are all busily doing the first in a very public way, and they have always tried to do the second. To achieve it they either have to show a specific

128

readership which may be small but is seen to be of direct interest to certain advertisers, or they have to increase their circulation. In so far as they opt for the latter course they are more and more likely to be politically bland and inoffensive. They can afford to give space to a writer well known to have different views because they reckon he will be swamped by the general tone of the paper. It also shows them in an impartial, objective light.

Facts and Comment

None of this is sinister, as the critics regularly imply. Once a paper's stance is understood, what it publishes can be readily evaluated. Nobody would expect *The Daily Telegraph* to espouse the cause of the Communist Party, or even of the Labour Party. At the same time it is important to accord due respect to its normal practice of reporting what its opponents say, even if the reporting is not really impartial. As earlier, once its principles are understood it is not difficult to assess the accuracy, fulness or balanced nature of its reporting.

If there are valid criticisms of daily paper reporting and comment on what are in the end political matters, they are to do with the difficulty at times of separating the two, and speed. The original guiding rule was 'facts are sacred, comment is free'. That was fine when it was possible to see easily which was which. It is now infinitely harder. Facts are chosen to make a point. Headlines are often written for effect and may not accurately reflect the content of the story. Pictures, especially of political figures, are regularly chosen to show them in either a flattering or demeaning light, according to the story and the paper's position. Issues are magnified beyond their real importance, again either to show how concerned or careless is the party promoting them. The instant rejoinder by journalists that 'We do not make the news, we only report what is happening' does not really suffice.

A further criticism is that the instant judgements called for by the need to publish the paper every day must be open to question. While there is no intrinsic merit in withholding judgement or comment, it is likely that some time for reflection will produce a better and possibly more balanced result. There are many examples. Statistics imperfectly analysed can be claimed to show that more young blacks are responsible for mugging old ladies than young whites. The instant comment that the situation clearly needs a return to public flogging or mass repatriation is easy to make but rather less than credible.

Of course there is no guarantee that comment made a week later would be any more acceptable or believable. But there is a fair chance that it would be.

The more specialized the subject, the more difficult it is for both writer and reader to understand enough to make or judge comment at speed. Even when the comments are made by specialists themselves – the National Farmers Union and the National Union of Agricultural Workers, say, on a matter affecting the agricultural industry – they are often drawn together by a journalist who may accidentally put the wrong emphasis into an interpretation. That can still be true even when the journalist has been writing on the industry for years. It is, after all, not uncommon for readers expert in something to find errors of both fact or assessment in the writings of would-be journalistic experts.

It is also almost impossible at times to define 'news' in a political context. An announcement that the police are to be given a salary increase is clearly news. The weaving into the stories then written that this will clearly assist recruitment and thus lead to a decrease in crime is comment written as news. And all readers will be familiar with the banal comments made by people who only justify space because they are well known. It is often difficult to see what is added to the reader's sum of knowledge to hear that Mr Bletherer MP agrees or disagrees with the decision to pay policemen more, a comment acquired by a paper because Mr Bletherer is adviser to the Burglars' Union. Few truer remarks have ever been made than 'he would, wouldn't he', but that has never stopped newspapers from pursuing the predictable.

It is also vital to distinguish the reality from the appearance. Entertaining writers like Julian Critchley are necessary – possibly required – reading. Books like Ken Livingstone's *If Voting Changed Anything They'd Abolish It* are also *de rigueur* for serious students. But articles and books need to be seen for what they are: sidelights based on a good deal of truth and experience but not the whole truth. Valuable comment describes them.

Television Arrives

Nevertheless it would be totally wrong to put newspapers in the dock and condemn them before studying the evidence carefully. Broadly speaking, British newspapers do report the national scene reasonably well. What finally saves the situation is that people really are free to buy from a range of publications not available in any other country. The press can rightly be accused of a paper-thin skin when faced with criticism, but then so can politicians.

All changed with the advent of television and its growth into the all-pervasive medium it is today. Television can be quite remarkably unmemorable but its general effect is undeniable. Whether in its factual, factional, or fictional work it is now so omnipresent that it is unrealistic to pretend that it does not shape attitudes. Critic Milton Shulman has regularly maintained that continual violence on the screen has helped to create the violent society of today. It may be an unprovable case but it is equally difficult to refute. It is acknowledged that some television programmes have altered society's views, e.g. about the homeless. Politically its influence is accepted all round. It is the medium from which most people get their daily fix of the big events of the day. It is the one for which politicians arrange their public appearances, in both senses of that word. It is the one politicians love to hate but cannot avoid.

It was said that when the late Lord Stockton was Prime Minister (as Harold Macmillan) he tried his hardest to avoid going on television, whether in news programmes or in studio events. He said his chances of losing were odds-on, his chances of drawing were no more than evens, and his chances of winning were negligible. If he made some comment he always had to have in mind how different people would hear it and interpret it, quite apart from those who would think he looked tired or too 'cocky' or devious. Yet he was one of the great performers.

The spoken word has the great benefit or drawback of the look of the person speaking, as well as the inflections he employs. Emotion is more easily or quickly conveyed on the screen than in the written word. The close-up can be the deadliest enemy of all. Newspapers can be and are edited, sometimes to the despair or rage of a politician. But there is a fairly well accepted right of reply and a reasonable chance that those who read the original will read the reply. This does not apply on television. Even if a politician were to be granted a return appearance on a fact-based series, there is no guarantee that those watching were watching before. Above all, television is obsessed with images. The government spokesman defending his party's record on housing will do so against a background of derelict slums or stockbroker belt mansions.

Newspaper writing has a permanence. The reader can go through an article, think about it, agree or disagree with the author, and at any time go back to it. Television does not permit this luxury, even with the ubiquitous video recorder.

Handling TV

Television also suffers badly from the 'I am the Almighty, don't you dare speak to me like that' syndrome. Apart from one astonishing case where the BBC capitulated before actually fighting its corner, neither of the two organizations has been renowned for admitting errors, either of fact or interpretation. Instead they normally rely on aggressive response, implying that the complainant is in some way unusual in not having understood and accepted the essentially fair programme or item.

The circumstances of production, particularly for studio programmes, compound the problems. Those about to be interviewed have to be at least partially made up, itself an unusual experience for most of them. The attempt to put them at their ease by offering them a drink in the hospitality room (sometimes dubbed the hostility room) is almost certainly doomed to failure – not that that is the fault of the hosts. The lights and total atmosphere of the studio make everything worse; then there is the interviewer . . . who is at least partly concerned with his/her own reputation and anxious to appear as the 'voice of the people'. Last of all there is either no audience other than the studio technicians, or the audience is like the crowd at a bullfight, waiting for the beast to die. Little wonder that many MPs, even though accustomed to public show and related not too distantly to actors, come out of the encounter badly.

Public figures must expect public scrutiny. They are not shrinking violets to be protected against the freezing stare of public opinion as seen through the eyes of the media. At the same time, while the media may have the divine duty to seek out the truth (questionable in itself and begging the question of what is the truth), it may not have the divine right to print it or screen it. That even allows for the dubious cover of the Official Secrets Act. There can be no doubt that a free society and a free press (which now of course includes television) go together. However, a free press cannot ignore its responsibilities. Sensation is a poor ally to put into the witness box. Page 3 girls are not news and are seldom even entertainment except of the most puerile kind. One salacious story that brings down a politician is not a justification for ill-founded gossip. Never forget that gossip sticks.

In the context of watching and influencing government, the media are open to attack in one particular aspect. It is the job of lobby correspondents to collect interpretation and explanation from ministers and MPs. It is understandable that on occasion the source of a comment may not wish to be revealed. The reasons may be reasonable or reprehensible but that is not important here. The government may wish to indicate its line of thinking while the opposition may wish to draw attention to aspects of proposed legislation or ministerial statements that the government has conveniently left out. In both instances identifying the source may lessen the impact of the comment. In the stately dance that is part of the political play neither may want to be seen too obviously. There is probably nothing wrong with that. Yet one part of the system is doubtful, to say the least. The lobby correspondents decided in 1986 to adhere to the regular background briefings by a non-person usually called 'sources close to the Prime Minister' or some similarly meaningless phrase. Only two daily newspapers refused to continue the practice.

Everybody knows that the 'source' is the Prime Minister's press officer, but the convention is that he should remain anonymous. It is part of the long-established love of secrecy in British society. It has little to commend it, and perhaps if the freedom of information campaign finally succeeds, it will be properly buried.

The role of the media at election time in reporting opinion polls has also been subjected to scrutiny (not always close) and fierce attack. Whether polls do influence opinion, however much they set out merely to reflect it, is probably unprovable. Nevertheless the record shows that the professionally conducted polls were consistently close to the actual result and in some cases exactly accurate. It is unlikely, to say the least, that in election results like the last two in Britain – 1983 and 1987 – where one party was so far ahead of the rest that published poll reports or forecasts would seriously shift intentions. It might have a bearing in the event of a hung Parliament, but there are far too many other factors at work to create that situation for polls to be the deciding one. In any event election time can only be usable for a pressure group, other organizations or individuals to try to wrest a promise about something from one candidate or a party. Once the election is over, the real bargaining begins and hastily considered remarks made in the heat of battle can be repudiated, denied, or, more likely, just ignored.

Good or bad, broadcasting and the press, because they are seen, heard and read in Westminster and Whitehall have an influence there which cannot be ignored. They can be used skilfully in support of a public affairs strategy. But if their coverage of an issue is adverse, that strategy is more likely to encounter difficulties with politicians and civil servants.

11

THE PROFESSIONALS

The 1986 Market & Opinion Research International (MORI) survey among MPs showed that many, on both sides of the House, recognized the need for organizations wishing to make or maintain contact with Parliament to have professional advice from lobbyists.

Harold Wilson called lobbying a 'degrading profession'. The Bow Group has said that lobbyists are performing a 'public service or are an expensive sham'. As Ian Picton of the Tory Reform Group tellingly remarked in an article in *PR Week*, the trade periodical: '. . . if you are lobbying on behalf of a social cause rather than a sectional interest . . . you cease to be a lobbyist and metamorphose into a campaigner'.

Public relations consultancies began to see a place for their talents in the monitoring of Parliament in the early 1950s. It grew into a more active operation in attempting to influence and change Parliamentary attitudes after a short time. Its description gradually moved from public relations to public affairs. The new phrase was explained by one distinguished practitioner, Tim Traverse-Healy, when he wrote: '. . . it describes the process whereby a company carefully considers the likely impact upon itself of possible political and social developments'. In the same issue of *PR Week* that carried the article by Mr Picton, ten consultancies advertised their services. One was a public relations agency, but the rest were specialists in this field. Four referred to public affairs and the other descriptions were

135

corporate affairs, political intelligence, political relations, political communication (which also happened to be in the firm's title), and government affairs.

It really does not matter what they are called: they are all undertaking the same kind of work. They all employ the same kind of people. They are not to be confused with the Society of Parliamentary Agents, whose members are lawyers.

Lobbyists, to use the most convenient term, began by differing from American practice – there are 6,000 registered lobbyists in the US – in one major respect. They tended to place more emphasis on monitoring than on traditional earbashing. Having warned their clients of something likely to happen that could be of concern, they introduced their clients to MPs and more or less left them to get on with it. That has changed and the consultants are now much more overt in their activities. There is admittedly a fine distinction between monitoring and lobbying but it is still there.

Also unlike the US the consultancies are not listed in an easily accessible register, though they must report their existence and the names of any MPs, MEPs, or persons elected to public office to The Institute of Public Relations, which does keep a register; and they also appear in the *Public Relations Year Book*, published by the *Financial Times* business services on behalf of the Public Relations Consultants Association. The only weakness is that not all consultants are members of the Institute, nor need they be registered consultants in the PRCA. MPs themselves are supposed to declare their business interests for the Register of MPs Interests (from the Stationery Office) but not all do this. There have been sporadic attempts in the House for a register to be set up but up to now no decision has been reached.

Lobbyists' Critics

When public relations as an organized activity was being established, it was regarded with intense suspicion. That has continued. Harold Wilson's comment has been noted. When its practitioners started appearing at Westminster, several MPs rang warning bells. They are still unconvinced. The backbench Labour MP Tam Dalyell claims that if he is approached by a lobbyist or consultancy he probably puts the phone down instantly or consigns a written approach to the waste paper basket. If he does decide to act, he goes to the principals of the lobbyist or consultant to check that they really do need help. It has to be said that he would probably be less likely to do this if it were a company or other organization in his constituency.

Not surprisingly the chief critics are more likely to be found in the Labour Party than in the Conservatives or Alliance. At the same time it is not uncommon to find Labour members more ready to try to understand business than those in the Conservative Party, who are sometimes guilty of the sin of pretending to know more than they really do. Certainly the MORI survey showed that the idea that the Labour Party was totally opposed to all private enterprise was hopelessly out of date.

From the MORI survey we find that more than one third of MPs found professionally manned agencies or company departments a useful source of information. Given the general request for information and briefing to be concise and succinct, it is not surprising that professional wordsmiths and students of human behaviour come into the picture.

In the end the work of the professionals is part of the 'who you know' syndrome, or possibly more accurately 'who you can get to know'. In addition, it means realizing that the Civil Service is often more important than MPs in the conception, origination, and initiation of new legislation.

When public relations professionals recognized the importance of Parliament and the Civil Service in their effect on business, they adapted the skills they had previously used in gaining editorial publicity or direct communication with key groups to the arcane rules of Parliament, and equally used them to break down the traditional reserve and secrecy of civil servants. At that stage without doubt many civil servants used the Official Secrets Act as a shelter from which they could claim they were unable to speak, listen or help. Both sides have moved nearer each other. Today's public affairs specialists, whether on the staff of an organization or acting as consultants, are often likely to be drawn from the ranks of former or even sitting members of both Houses, civil servants who have retired or resigned, or those who have been political aides or researchers.

Even so, the organizations that use their services are not entirely sure of their value. Another survey, this time undertaken by an anonymous group, revealed that 61 per cent of the companies questioned saw a need for using consultants to monitor Parliament, a figure rising to 69 per cent when it came to monitoring Whitehall. Ninety-two per cent looked for early warning about policies and 59 per cent wanted advice on the action to take. Thirty-one per cent expected the consultancies to act as their spokesmen in the process of contact and influence.

Interestingly enough a brief survey in Washington, reported in *Fortune Magazine*, recorded a broadly held view among senators and congressmen that they were 'impressed when corporate chieftains, rather than hired lobbying guns, come calling. Says one business lobbyist: 'Legislators know that the commitment of a professional lobbyist to an issue is only as deep as his current client's.' Unkind perhaps, but worth remembering. British attitudes may not be that different and indeed there are some notable business heads who are familiar faces around Westminster and Whitehall, assiduous in putting their company's case. There is here a touch of the British love of the amateur: in this context one who keeps his contact with government going as a part, but only a part (however important), of his job. The suspicion of the full-time professional that undoubtedly exists in Britain easily surfaces as a view of the consultant.

In the anonymous survey cited here it was noticeable that, despite the acceptance of the need for consultants, only 8 per cent of the respondents thought their outside advisers were useful in providing access to the real decision-makers in Whitehall. Twenty-eight per cent thought that too much of the consultants' effort was aimed at Parliament, since there were reservations about whether they really had sufficient knowledge or experience of the inner workings of the Civil Service. Andrew Roth, the political journalist and author, is on record as saying that lobbyists are prey to boastfulness and deceit in their claims, trading on the naiveté of their clients. He is almost certainly right since this is a field in which *caveat emptor* applies all the time, but probably even nearer the truth is the former civil servant who was quoted as saying: 'They don't always win and it isn't right that they should. But their case does not go by default'. Perhaps Roth's judgement is over-hard, for there can be no disputing that the professional operators of the present are very professional indeed.

Skill and Common Sense

The professionals exercise a delicate role in advising their employers or clients. While some can record notable successes to go with the failures, most would probably claim that they did not necessarily change policies or impending legislation but that they helped materially to make it workable. It is an unfortunate fact in the latter part of the twentieth century that some legislation, while laudable in its ambition, fails because there are not enough officials to police it, to see that it is observed. Being sensitive to the subtleties (which is why it is always better to hire a native of the country than a foreigner), they instinctively understand that the business of influence does mean a two-way process. There is a time to speak and a time to listen; and when listening, there is the overriding need to be seen to hear. In what has been called this 'mysterious, complex and muddled area' the skill of the negotiator has to be at its highest, and the constant practice of the professional sharpens nicely. Michael Thomas, the former MP now working as a Parliamentary consultant, says: 'Most lobbyists do nothing a member of the public could not do. They just know how to do it'. It was a fairly simple statement but still hid the essential value of an experienced executive making analyses and value judgements full-time.

Consultants are always in the business of seeking more clients. It is thus not surprising that many have set down their approach to the job. One of them argued that the two necessary elements to successful working were 'a sensitive and efficient intelligence service' and the 'development of contacts'. She also pointed out that even if an organization such as a trade association or professional institute was 'strongly committed' to a cause, and was determined to lobby on behalf of its members, there is still an important role for individual companies to play in reinforcing the message:

> Institutions can give the overview, but there is nothing so compelling as the impact that can be made by individual companies. They are at the sharp end and can speak with authority as employers, producers, marketers and risk-takers. . . . it is in the long-term interests of both business and government that they should understand each other's worlds. Increasingly, each impinges on the other.

The case for using outside advisers is not difficult to make. They have experience, they have time, they lower unit costs because they can spread them among several clients, and they know what they are doing.

The chairman of one major British company said: 'If you don't lobby, the government assumes you have no problems'.

Codes of practice

There is still that strong suspicion of the activities of the professionals in the Houses of Parliament. There are those who believe that plain envelopes stuffed with fivers change hands in dark corners. There are others who believe the practice of the American Political Action Committee holds sway in Britain. The PACs came into being in the 1970s, and permit individuals or organizations to make direct contributions to candidates and sitting senators and congressmen, in return for which they get a hearing. The scale of the custom is staggering. In 1985 twenty-seven US senators accepted almost $10 million from PACs. One actually keeps a computer print-out handy to remind him of those to whom he is indebted.

While it is right to be on guard – some of the individuals and firms in this field are considerably less than ethical or honest – most of the practitioners are well above board. Nothing like the PACs is likely to happen here, even if our MPs are really badly underpaid and overworked.

Reputable firms will observe the codes of conduct or practice issued by the Institute of Public Relations and Public Relations Consultants Association. A company looking to retain a consultancy or a company wishing to employ an individual specialist ought to go to these two bodies. Those wanting a rapid guide to what professionals do and how they view their task would be well advised to buy a copy of *Lobbying in the British Parliament*, published in 1986 and written by two senior practitioners, Arthur Butler and Douglas Smith.

In their introduction the authors remind the reader that exercising influence takes time and includes contact with more bodies than MPs or civil servants. As they say: '. . . if you arrive at the point when all stands or falls on an occasion at Westminster, then very likely your case has been either advanced too late or too ineptly at a far earlier stage in the process'. Another experienced specialist in this area had the same thought in different words: 'If you need to mount a campaign on a particular issue it means you are too late and will probably fail'.

Butler and Smith also provide one of the most indispensable pieces of advice when they write: 'Working in the Palace of Westminster calls for a particular sensitivity just as much as having a good case to argue. It also requires patience and flexibility because the one golden rule for lobbying Parliament is that there is no golden rule'. More than 20 years ago an early master of the craft wrote:

There is no book that tells just what is allowed and what is an outrage, but to do the wrong thing can cause great offence and is a sure and certain mark of ignorance. MPs do not much care for those who do not understand the niceties of behaviour at Westminster. Good behaviour is step number one on the tightrope that joins Parliament and public relations.

Butler and Smith's version of this is:

> Quite apart from building goodwill and contacts for the future amongst rising MPs, or for that matter with senior, former Ministers who still have good contacts and advice to offer there is the great advantage of access. MPs have a 'feel' for the House, how a case is properly presented to it, and who should best be approached. They can also gain necessary information more quickly, or speed the passage of a delegation to those who are most able to assist. First, however, they must be convinced of the rightness of a client's case, which is why any initial meetings are so vital. It is a hurdle where, sadly, too many fall flat upon their faces.

Nothing really changes!

Be Ever Watchful

From a mass of sound, practical advice, three extracts are pertinent:

> The arguments you advance should be mature. No-one serious in government will deny anyone their right to advance a view or push their case. They will recognize how self interest, as well as some national interest, will equally be behind such moves. But legislators, whether professional or elected, must see any argument in a wider perspective. They will take account not only of existing resources but also of other pressures or policy lines. Any strident proposals will be as scantily considered as a product press release over-ripe with adjectives and excessive claims.

Commenting on the skills a professional adviser brings to his job, especially in creating an information base, Butler and Smith emphasize the need to be aware of what is going on as soon as possible:

The earlier one can spot an idea or policy developing, the easier it is to block it or amend it. The first sign might be a resolution for a party conference, which could lead to a debate which in turn could lead to a resolution going before a party policy making committee preparing material for the election manifesto. By the time the proposal has been polished and published in a government White Paper, it is that much more difficult to deal with. Once it has appeared in a Bill it is even more difficult to tackle. So the best advice to the fisher for political information is: 'Cast your net wide and cast it early'.

Companies who can afford the services of professional consultants will have taken this advice to heart. But even small companies who feel the cost beyond them can learn.

Butler and Smith echo the words of the consultant of 20 years ago when they warn:

> There have been some hair-raising examples of clumsy claims in the past, which seemed designed to lead the ignorant potential client to believe that the consultant had some magic or other power over MPs or civil servants. It should be remembered that anyone suggesting he has some power which will ensure that parliamentary questions will be tabled, motions signed, bills introduced, or Select Committee enquiries set up is laying himself open to the charge that he has committed a breach of Parliamentary privilege. Naturally, the Commons is very touchy about any suggestion that honourable members can be 'bought'.

A Register Needed

The PRCA believes that there is an overwhelming case for a proper register of consultants or lobbyists. The objections to their very existence, usually from well meaning, idealistic members who feel the House is being suborned to the wicked and venal interests of commercial companies, are unreal. In this world information is the key to all progress. If consultants can sit in the middle, relaying information to both sides in a debate or argument, they are playing a valuable role. It they are asked to be ashamed of it, they are bound to devise underhand means and methods of plying their trade. Better that all should be open and above board, though that need not mean going as far as the Americans.

John Heddle, the Conservative MP, remarked once that lobbying is a subtle and sophisticated art that can only be effectively executed by people who understand the machinery of government, who understand the interface between Whitehall and Westminster, and who comprehend the relation between government and industry. That should not be interpreted to mean that only professionals can be successful. Careful assimilation of the obvious rules, coupled with advice from the constitutency MP and a relevant civil servant, can often set the harassed small business owner or manager on the right path. That in no way decries the professional, but it has to be remembered that many people's resources are limited.

Finally it is worth pondering the likely effect of a hung Parliament. This could be a real minefield, where the professional would come into his own. Reconciling different interests, balancing conflicts, and above all forecasting trade-offs would need the best of skills. In the process democracy and freedom might be well served.

12

HELP WHEN YOU
NEED IT

Advice and constructive help are never far away – and often free.

To be aware of what is going through the government's mind, or that of the Opposition, or even that of individual members, does take time and effort. It is for the person acting on his own, or for an organization that wishes to raise its voice, to decide how much time and effort is worth expending, but neither can complain of lacking either advice or help.

In a world almost drowning in paper, Parliament would not wish to be excluded – so it is not. Advance warning of thought processes comes from newspapers, either officially ('The Government proposes to introduce legislation in the next session etc. etc.') or unofficially ('The Government is thought to be considering etc. etc.'). Naturally one does not expect to find too much of this sort of material in *The Sun* or the *News of the World*, so one has to turn to the 'quality' dailies and Sundays. Flashing signals can also be picked up in weeklies like *The Economist* or *The Spectator*. Just as water will eventually find its way into every nook and cranny so will a piece of leaked information, so that it is worth keeping an eye on influential weeklies like *New Scientist*. The only trouble is that by the time something appears in them it may be getting almost too late. But they should not be missed.

At a later stage the Government may plunge in with a green paper, which is a way of floating an idea to see what reaction it produces. Depending on that, the idea is either dropped, amended, or later presented as a firm proposal in a white paper. There is a method between the two known as a white paper with green edges, in which the government states an intention but does not actually promise legislation. That allows it to withdraw gracefully if opposition suddenly builds up.

The Opposition parties make their points by publishing statements, discussion papers and even books.

Official papers are obtainable from Her Majesty's Stationery Office, which has offices in London, Edinburgh, Manchester, Bristol, Birmingham and Belfast.

Guides to party thinking are available from their headquarters.

The Conservative and Unionist Central Office is at 32 Smith Square, London, SW1P 3HH.

The Labour Party is at 150 Walworth Road, London, SE17 1JT.

The SLD is at 1 Whitehall Place, London, SW1A 2HE.

The Social Democratic Party is at 4 Cowley Street, London, SW1.

The minor parties, such as Scottish Nationalists, Ulster Unionists, Plaid Cymru, are listed in the telephone book.

In many cases of course it is best to start with the local MP. If it is a non-party constituency matter, he or she will at least start things going. If it is a party matter or in some other way contentious, e.g. one would hardly ask an avowed left-winger to support an idea about privatization or a right-wing member to argue for more powers for trade unions, it may be better to go to the party headquarters. It is also entirely feasible to discover the hopefuls waiting in the wings for the next election. They will be anxious to promote themselves and may prove useful. The local paper will provide the name, or it can be found through the local office of the party concerned, which will be in the telephone book.

Information about the House itself – its work, its methods, what is allowed and not allowed in approaching Members of either House – can be readily had from the Journal and Information Office of the House of Lords, or the Public

Information Office of the Commons – both extremely helpful. Records and documents can be inspected by application to the Clerk of the Records, in the House of Lords.

The final arbiter of proceedings in the House is the Speaker, but for a brief guide consult the *Manual of Procedure in the Public Business*, from the Stationery Office. Serious students would need to get immersed in Erskine May, the Bible of Parliament, correctly called the *Law, Privileges, Proceedings and Usage of Parliament*, originally by Sir Erskine May but now updated. Although important, these books are not strictly necessary for the task of trying to influence Parliament.

For a straightforward listing of the Members of both Houses, the composition of government, key people in all parties, national organizations and public offices and so on *Vacher's Parliamentary Companion*, corrected each quarter, is invaluable. Even more comprehensive, because it includes such things as explanations of Parliamentary terms and biographical details of members of both Houses, is *Dod's Parliamentary Companion*, published each year anew. After an election, it is wise to buy *The Times Guide to the House of Commons*.

The CBI booklet 'Working with Politicians' is a useful brief guide covering national, local and European politics. Updated from time to time, it also gives some practical advice on the value and problems of guiding employees who have political aspirations. From the CBI at Centre Point, 103 New Oxford Street, London, WC1A 1DU. Throughout each session *The House Magazine* is essential reading and especially closely followed by Members.

It is naturally more difficult to divine the ways civil servants are thinking, but since much legislation starts with them, it is correspondingly more important to try to find out. It is probably best to establish who in the sponsoring department (that is the department of state taking responsibility for whatever particular area of activity is concerned) is the key official. It would be naive, to put it at its mildest, to expect that official to reveal openly and instantly what is being considered, but there is nothing to prevent anybody registering a view or making a point. Unlike in years past, and not in accord with popular opinion, civil servants are very ready to listen and be helpful. A guide to who is who is the *Civil Service Year Book*, from the Stationery Office. Names of the most senior people are in *Vacher's* and *Dod's*.

Another CBI booklet 'Working with Whitehall' is also valuable, particularly for its listing of sponsoring ministries, for a long list of industry sectors with the division responsible within each ministry, and addresses. Even if the nature of the Department of Trade and Industry changes under pressure from its minister, the listings are still a useful starting point.

The European Commission has offices at 8 Storey's Gate, London, SW1P 3AT; at 7 Alva Street, Edinburgh, EH2 4PH; at 4 Cathedral Road, Cardiff, CF1 9SG; and Windsor House, 9/15 Bradford Street, Belfast BT2 7EG.

The European Parliament has its London office at 2 Queen Anne's Gate, London SW1H 2AA.

A useful directory to see if there is a trade association, institute, or some other body interested in a particular subject is the *Directory of British Associations*, from CBD Research, Beckenham, Kent, whose staff are extremely helpful on the telephone. The Macmillan directory *The European Community* is packed with relevant information. Given the inevitability of some out-dated details, a problem faced by all annuals or periodical directories, one of its special values is its listing of the representative organizations for industries, retail trade and the professions. Available from Globe Book Services, Houndmills, Basingstoke, Hants RG21 2XS.

Lastly, The Institute of Public Relations is at Gate House, 1 St John's Square, London, EC1M 4DH, and the Public Relations Consultants Association is at 10 Belgrave Square, London, SW1X 8PH.

BIBLIOGRAPHY

As a rule bibliographies are included to demonstrate how well read the author has been, and from how many other writers he has drawn evidence or inspiration. This is no less true of me. However, the list that follows is intended to supplement the practical advice as well as to indicate some books that serious students of the subject might like to consult. I have deliberately, here and in the rest of the book, tried to avoid personal memoirs. They tend to be false witnesses, and those who wish to read them to confirm or deny their own prejudices need no encouragement from me.

Any harvester in the field of government needs to be familiar with:

Butler, Arthur and Smith, Douglas, *Lobbying in the British Parliament*, PRCA, 1986.
Civil Service Year Book.
Directory of the Commission of the European Communities.
Dod's Parliamentary Companion.
Government & Industry – a business guide to Westminster, Whitehall and Brussels, Kluwer Publishing.
House Magazine, The
Register of Members' Interests, The
Times Guide to the House of Commons, The
Vacher's Parliamentary Companion (corrected quarterly)

Those who want to go further into the subject could do worse than read:

Alderman, Geoffrey, *Pressure Groups and Government in Great Britain*, Longman, 1984.

Birch, Anthony H., *The British System of Government*, 7th edn, London: Allen & Unwin, 1986.

Brown R. G. S., Steel D. R., *The Administrative Process in Britain*, 2nd edn, Methuen, 1983.

Chapman, Leslie, *Your Disobedient Servant*, Penguin, 1979.

Coxall W. N., *Parties and Pressure Groups*, 2nd edn, Longman, 1986.

Dunleavy P., Husbands C. P., *British Democracy at the Crossroads*, London: Allen & Unwin, 1985.

Grant, Wyn with Jane Sargent, *Business and Politics in Britain*, Macmillan, 1987.

Hamer, Mick, *Wheels within Wheels – a study of the road today.* Routledge and Kegan Paul, 1987.

Kellner, Peter and Crowther-Hunt, Lord, *The Civil Servants*, London: Macdonald, 1980.

Lifting the Lid on Lobbying, Local Government Information Unit, 1986.

Moran, Michael, *Politics and Society in Britain*, Macmillan, 1985.

Ponting, Clive, *Whitehall: Tragedy or Farce*, Hamish Hamilton, 1986.

Pym, Bridget, *Pressure Groups and the Permissive Society*, David & Charles, 1974.

Richards, Peter G., *Mackintosh's The Government and Politics of Britain*, 6th edn, London: Hutchinson, 1985.

Robertson, David, *The Dictionary of Politics*, Penguin, 1985.

Walkland S. A., Ryle, Michael, eds., *The Commons Today*, Fontana, 1981.

INDEX